# WILDFLOWEI

## OF THE

# NORTH YORKSHIRE COAST

## Nan Sykes

*Photographs by the author*

Photo by Mike Kipling

NAVE-NORTRAIL
The North Sea Trail

*Wildflowers of the Yorkshire Coast* has been produced with funding from the Nortrail Project which is creating a walking trail around the countries of the North Sea – Norway, Sweden, Denmark, Germany and the Netherlands, as well as England and Scotland.

Nortrail links walking opportunities with the rich, and often common, natural and cultural heritage of the North Sea countries.

Published by the North York Moors National Park Authority

ISBN 1 904622 02 X

# CONTENTS

| | 2–4 petals | 5 or more petals | | composite | | peaflower |
|---|---|---|---|---|---|---|
| **WHITE** | scurvygrass 32 whitlowgrass 33 bittercress 33 holly 34 bedstraws 34 cleavers 34 garlic mustard 32 enchanters nightshade 32 shepherds purse 33 horseradish 32 hoarycress 32 swinecress 33 thalecress 33 privet 34 woodruff 34 watercress 33 | dropwort 40 anemone 40 blackthorn 35 guelder rose 35 cherry 35 bramble 36 burnet rose 36 corn spurrey 36 brookweed 38 campions 38 chickweeds 39 white bryony 37 crowfoot 37 stitchworts 39 blinks 37 spring beauty 37 | meadowsweet 40 ramsons 40 hawthorn 35 elder 35 crab apple 35 raspberry 36 rowan 36 fairy flax 36 wood sorrel 36 strawberry 38 mouse-ear 39 sandworts 37 stonecrop 37 grass of Parnassus 38 | rnayweeds 41 daisies 41 yarrow 41 sneezewort 41 feverfew 41 | | clover 44 white melilot 64 |
| **GREEN BROWN** | lady's mantle 69 pearlwort 45 | black bryony 45 | | | | |
| **YELLOW CREAM** | spurge laurel 52 wintercress 53 tormentil 52 cabbage 53 wallflower 52 golden saxifrage 52 moschatel 68 mustard 53 lady's bedstraw 52 crosswort 52 charlock 53 rocket 53 | wood avens 55 silverweed 54 buttercups 54 cowslip 55 agrimony 56 barberry 55 St John's wort 57 stonecrop 57 celandine 58 gooseberry 55 | yellow pimpernel 57 cinquefoil 54 primrose 55 mullein 56 marsh marigold 56 wall lettuce 55 pansies 56 yellow wort 58 rockrose 56 spearwort 54 | coltsfoot 61 goldenrod 61 leopardsbane 60 carline thistle 60 dandelion 62 sowthistles 62 hawksbeards 63 hawkbits 63 nipplewort 61 pineappleweed 59 | fleabane 61 gumplant 61 groundsels 59 goatsbeard 62 hawkweeds 62 tansy 59 oxtongue 61 catsear 63 ragworts 60 | gorse 64 broom 64 dyers greenweed 64 melilot 64 kidney vetch 64 trefoils 65 medicks 65 vetchling 65 |
| **RED** | poppy 70 | montbretia 70 scarlet pimpernel 70 | | | | clovers 71 |
| **MAUVE PINK PURPLE** | cuckoo flower 74 willowherbs 73 speedwells 89 field madder 74 sea rocket 74 danish scurvygrass 32 honesty 74 dames violet 74 gentian 74 | storksbill 75 herb robert 75 spurreys 76 ragged robin 76 sea milkwort 75 red campion 76 thrift 81 gentian 74 violets 88 loosestrife 82 | cranesbills 75 mallow 76 valerians 78 marsh violet 88 roses 76 centaury 75 crab apple 35 bittersweet 88 Duke of Argyll's teaplant 88 | knapweed 79 sawwort 79 scabious 79 thistles 80 | | restharrow 83 everlasting pea 83 vetches 83 |
| **BLUE** | speedwells 89 | green alkanet 91 meadow cranesbill 91 forgetmenots 90 | | sea aster 90 chicory 90 | | tare 83 |

| bell | lipped flower | cluster or umbel | spike | flower Irregular or obscure | |
|---|---|---|---|---|---|
| bindweed 40<br>lily of the valley 40<br>snowdrop 40 | deadnettle 44<br>hempnettle 44 | cow parsley 42<br>chervil 42<br>upright hedge parsley 42<br>hemlock 42<br>sweet cicely 42<br>carrot 42<br>water dropwort 42<br>hogweed 43<br>angelica 43<br>celery 43<br>burnet saxifrage 44<br>pignut 44<br>ground elder 43<br>sanicle 44<br>water parsnip 43<br>fools watercress 43 | pale persicaria 72 | eyebright 44<br>knotgrass 44<br>fumitory 78<br>milkwort 91 | **WHITE** |
| | | | reedmace 47<br>plantains 66<br>arrowgrass 51<br>docks 72 | frog orchid 47  twayblade 47<br>oraches 46  fat-hen 46<br>arrowgrass 51  nettles 45<br>saltwort 46  reeds 47<br>horsetails 48  sedges 51<br>dogs mercury 45  parsley piert 45<br>rushes 48, 50, 51  grasses 49, 50 | **GREEN BROWN** |
| | yellow archangel 69 | alexanders 53<br>pepper saxifrage 58<br>parsley 58 | plantains 66<br>mugwort 67<br>weld 67<br>mignonette 67<br>woodsage 67<br>sea beet 67<br>toadflax 67 | daffodil 69  hazel 68<br>corydalis 66  spurge 68<br>ivy 68  cudweed 68<br>honeysuckle 69  hayrattte 69<br>goldilocks 54  yellow flag iris 69 | **YELLOW CREAM** |
| | | | redshank 72<br>sorrels 72<br>docks 72 | figworts 71  sea buckthorn 70<br>red valerian 70  burnets 71<br>hazel 68  lords and ladies 70 | **RED** |
| bilberry 84<br>heathers 84<br>foxglove 84<br>bindweed 84<br>comfrey 84 | deadnettles 85<br>woundwort 86<br>red bartsia 85<br>black horehound 85<br>lousewort 85<br>betony 86<br>basil 85<br>orchids 77, 78<br>balsam 85<br>selfheal 86<br>bugle 86<br>ground ivy 86<br>clary 86<br>calamint 85 | hedge parsley 81<br>marjoram 81<br>hemp agrimony 81<br>valerians 78<br>burdock 81<br>butterburs 81<br>teasel 81<br>mint 82<br>thrift 81 | bistort 82<br>hoary plantain 82<br>bridewort 82<br>loosestrife 82<br>mint 82<br>toadflax 82 | milkwort 91<br>fumitory 78<br>pellitory-of-the-wall 87<br>ivy-leaved toadflax 87<br>butterwort 87<br>small toadflax 87<br>crowberry 84<br>toothwort 87<br>thyme 87<br>orchids 77, 78 | **MAUVE PINK** |
| bellfower 91<br>harebell 91<br>bluebell 91<br>comfrey 84 | | | | milkwort 91 | **BLUE** |

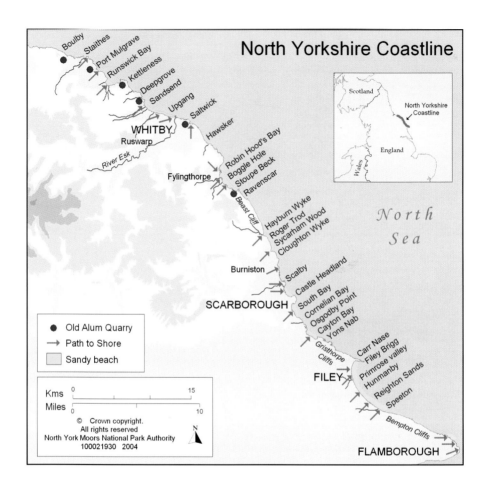

# North Yorkshire Coastline

Boulby
Staithes
Port Mulgrave
Runswick Bay
Kettleness
Deepgrove
Sandsend
Upgang
Saltwick
WHITBY
Ruswarp
Hawsker
River Esk
Robin Hood's Bay
Boggle Hole
Stoupe Beck
Fylingthorpe
Ravenscar
Beast Cliff
Hayburn Wyke
Roger Trod
Sycarham Wood
Cloughton Wyke
Burniston
Scalby
Castle Headland
South Bay
SCARBOROUGH
Cornelian Bay
Osgodby Point
Cayton Bay
Yons Nab
Gristhorpe Cliffs
Carr Nase
Filey Brigg
Primrose valley
Hunmanby
FILEY
Reighton Sands
Speeton
Bempton Cliffs
FLAMBOROUGH

North Sea

Scotland

North Yorkshire Coastline

England

Wales

## Legend

- ● Old Alum Quarry
- → Path to Shore
- ▢ Sandy beach

Kms  0 — 15
Miles 0 — 10

N

# INTRODUCTION

This book is intended as a handy field guide for people who enjoy being out and about in the countryside and would like to name and understand a little more about wildflowers they see, but have neither the time nor inclination for lengthy botanical study. Without the perplexity of an in-depth flora covering the whole of Britain or the inclination to unravel technical jargon, this guide should enable the naming of most flowering plants growing along the coast between Flamborough headland and Boulby cliff north of Staithes. It covers wildflowers growing on shores, cliff slopes and cliff tops back to cultivated land. Many can be seen from the Cleveland Way (North Sea Trail), the Wolds Way and other footpaths in the area. Cliff slopes can be hazardous places to explore but most of their plants can also be seen from the shore or cliff top paths. Strandline plants which grow only in sea spray on tidal beaches are best enjoyed with an awareness of high water times – it is advisable to leave small bays and most shores at least 2 hours before high tide.

The range and location of species covered are based on searches made by the author assisted by colleagues: Marjorie Anderson, Margaret Atherden, Jenny Bartlett, Pauline Bastow, Cedric Gillings, Dave Green, Jo Johnson,Tamar Jones, Vincent Jones, Pam Lawe, Jill Magee, Mavis Readman, Alan Hitson, Sylvia Robinson, Ken Trewren, Chris Wilson, Pat Wood and Mike Yates. I am grateful for their help and encouragement, exploring many miles of exposed cliffs in all weathers and recording plants on some rewarding (and occasionally daunting) flower-rich sites. Valuable technical and editorial advice was given by Anne Dennier, Kendrick Hutchinson and Gill Smith. I would also like to acknowlege assistance from the North York Moors National Park, the Nortrail Project, the National Trust, English Nature and the Heritage Coast project.

The book provides a simplified means of identification based on flower colour and form while limiting selection only to species known to occur locally. The colour and flower shape key inside the front cover is a useful starting point, followed by a search through the picture section. Remember that flower hue can vary somewhat, especially in the pink-mauve-purple-blue range, and that some normally bright coloured species occasionally produce white flowered specimens. If the query plant is difficult to trace, try an adjacent colour section. Check also the flower structure – split and lobed petals can be misleading; closely packed small flowers may be categorised as clusters or umbels – or by petal numbers if easily seen.The flowering time chart and species description should provide further help towards naming your plant.

*restharrow*

## FLOWER IDENTIFICATION

Naming a flower is not too difficult provided its salient features are noted. Instead of a quick glance at 'a pretty pink flower' a mental note of some of the following characteristics followed by reference to the species section should help to solve most queries.

| | |
|---|---|
| *HABITAT* | light or shady, ground wet, dry, bare, grassy, woody, sandy, rocky |
| *NEARBY PLANTS* | type of surrounding vegetation<br>is the query plant growing alone or in a colony? |
| *MONTH IN FLOWER* | |
| *PLANT FORM* | erect spike, spreading ground cover, clustered, climbing, shrubby, flimsy, branched, sticky, fragrant, prickly etc |
| *HEIGHT & WIDTH* | approximate overall plant size and shape |
| *FLOWER* | colour (can be variable), size, shape, approx number per stem |
| *PETALS* | number per flower, matching or irregular, spurred, notched etc |
| *SEPALS* | number, spreading or tubular, absent |
| *STEMS* | round, square, winged, ridged, hairy or glabrous, spiny, hollow |
| *LEAVES* | shape, size, in opposite pairs or spaced up stems, stalked or not, ground rosette; toothed, lobed or smooth edged<br>hairs – on top and/or below, felted, shiny, fleshy, rough, smooth |

## PLANT STRUCTURE

**A flower** consists of male stamens with anthers producing pollen and a female stigma which receives pollen to fertilise seeds; these are contained in an ovary and eventually disperse to grow into new plants. Most (but not all) flowers have coloured petals to attract pollinating insects and outer usually green sepals which protect a flower in bud. To ensure survival of the species flowers have evolved a vast range of features to maximise seed production, pollination, dispersal and germination – hence the bewildering variation of flower, fruit and plant forms.

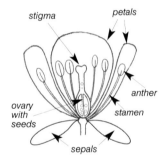

**Leaf shape** varies both between species and quite often on a single plant eg harebell has almost round lower leaves in early summer but very different linear leaves later. Many species have a ground rosette of leaves quite unlike those growing from the stem. Leaf shape and texture are a guide to a plant's identity.

**Stems** may be round, square, or have 2 or 4 raised vertical ridges with or without wings; sedges are triangular in cross section; grasses may be round or flattish.

*pinnate*  *lobed*  *trifoliate*  *simple and toothed*

*ridged*  *round winged striated*

*square*  *triangular*

| | |
|---|---|
| *alternate (foliage)* | leaves growing alternately from each side of a stem |
| *annual* | a plant which grows, flowers, seeds and dies back in 12 months |
| *anther* | a sac containing pollen, grows at the end of a stamen |
| *auricle* | projections which clasp a stem at the base of a leaf |
| *awn* | a projecting bristle frequent in grasses; at leaf end on some other species. |
| *base-rich* | refers to soils rich in alkaline nutrients |
| *beaked* | end projection resembling a birdís beak eg geranium fruits |
| *biennial* | a plant which requires two seasons to complete its life cycle |
| *bog* | wet acid peat usually with sphagnum moss and moorland plants |
| *bract* | a small leaf at the base of leaf stalk and on some flower stems |
| *calyx* | collection of sepals forming outer ring of flower parts; may be fused into a tube |
| *composite* | refers to a daisy type flowerhead with many tiny florets closely packed |
| *cordate* | describes a heart-shaped leaf base |
| *disc florets* | in a composite flowerhead, tiny tubed petalless flowers which form a dense central disc |
| *floret* | a tiny flower in a composite flowerhead |
| *flower* | consists of a female stigma(s) growing from a seed-filled ovary, pollen-producing male stamens and usually surrounded by petals and sepals |
| *flush* | ground kept wet by seeping spring water |
| *glabrous* | without hairs |
| *gland* | small swelling on flower or foliage which secretes juice, sometimes sticky |
| *glaucous* | bluish/grey colour of foliage instead of green |
| *halophyte* | a plant adapted to living in sea-salt environment |
| *introduced* | indicates a plant arrived here by human activity rather than natural forces |
| *irregular* | an asymetrical arrangement of flower parts |
| *keel* | the lower 2 petals of pea-type flowers, also grass leaves, folded like a boat keel |
| *latex* | a milky juice contained in some stems |
| *leaflets* | small leaves attached to a main leaf stalk |
| *linear* | describes a narrow parallel sided leaf |
| *lip* | the lower, often larger or notched lower petal of some irregular flowers |
| *marsh* | wet ground not on peat |
| *perennial* | a plant which lives for more that 2 years |
| *pollen* | minurte often yellow grains dispersed from anthers to fertilise seeds |
| *ray florets* | in a composite flowerhead, tiny flowers which have a single petal or ray |
| *reflexed* | bent abruptly backwards |
| *sepals* | small often green pointed leaves below or around flower petals |
| *simple* | describes a leaf not divided into leaflets |
| *spadix* | in wild arum, a finger-like projection which attracts pollinating insects |
| *spathe* | a large bract enfolding part of a flower |
| *spike* | erect plant with numerous flowers closely packed around the upper stem |
| *spikelet* | a grass 'seed' composed of bracts enclosing ovary, stigma and stamens |
| *spur* | small narrow or cone-like projection from petal or sepal, often contains nectar |
| *stamen* | male flower part comprising thin stalk or filament supporting pollen filled anther |
| *standard* | upper and usually upright petal of pea-type flowers |
| *stigma* | sticky tip of female flower style, able to receive pollen |
| *stipule* | leafy or scaly growth at junction of leaf stalk and main stem |
| *striated* | marked with long narrow channels or ridges |
| *strandline* | upper shore where tides turn leaving accumulation of debris |
| *tepals* | a flower part when petals and sepals are alike eg in rushes |
| *trifoliate* | a leaf with 3 leaflets eg clover |
| *umbel* | flat or dome-shaped head of small flowers on stems radiating like umbrella spokes from a central stem |
| *wart* | small tubercle on dock and sorrel tepals turning red as fruit ripens |
| *whorl* | leaflets or flowers arranged like a ruff or circular collar round a stem |
| *wings* | on pea-type flowers, the two side petals between upright standard and low keel |
| *winged stem* | a stem with 2, 3 or 4 vertical flanges |

# FLOWERING TIMES

Most species have an optimum time of flowering. This can help their identification, but normal timing can be affected by weather and by a sheltered or an exposed location. A few adaptable plants are able to flower during any month in the year although they are usually less prolific during the winter period; some species flower for only 2-3 weeks yet other species continue to flower for months.

## NORMAL START OF MAIN FLOWERING PERIOD

| | | | | | | |
|---|---|---|---|---|---|---|
| **jan** | coltsfoot | hazel | snowdrop | spurge laurel | whitlowgrass | winter heliotrope |
| **feb** | barren strawberry | blackthorn butterbur | celandine daffodil | dogs mercury gooseberry | moschatel primrose | violets |
| **mar** | dandelion ground ivy | lords and ladies red campion | speedwells | marsh marigold | violets | wallflower |
| **apr** | alexanders bilberry bitter vetch bittercress bluebell broom bugle buttercups | cow parsley cowslip crosswort cuckoo flower early purple orchid forgetmenot garlic mustard | goldilocks greater stitchwort herb robert hogweed honesty kidney vetch lousewort | marsh violet medicks mouse-ear Oxford ragwort pansies plantains ramsons scurvygrass | spring beauty spurges storksbill thalecress thrift toothwort vetches water crowfoot | white deadnettle wild cherry wild strawberry wood anemone wood sorrel woodruff |
| **may** | arrowgrass barberry black bryony bladder campion bramble burnet rose butterwort charlock cleavers clovers comfrey | corydalis crowberry crab apple cranesbills dames violet dropwort fairy flax field madder fumitory goatsbeard green alkanet hawkweeds | hawthorn hayrattle hedge mustard hoary cress holly ivy-lvd toadflax leopardsbane lily-of-the- valley mayweed meadow vetchling | milkwort ox-eye daisy pennycress pignut pineappleweed ragged robin rockrose rough chervil rowan salad burnet sanicle sea sandwort | silverweed sorrels speedwells spurrey stitchworts stonecrop sweet cicely thyme tormentil trefoils marsh valerian watercress | white bryony wild cabbage wood avens yellow archangel yellow pimpernel |
| **jun** | agrimony bedstraw betony bindweeds bistort bittersweet black horehound brookweed catsear centaury chicory cinquefoil clary docks Duke of Argyll's teaplant | dyers greenweed eastern rocket elder enchanters nightshade everlasting pea eyebright fat-hen feverfew figwort fools water- cress foxglove grass of Parnassus great burnet | ground elder guelder rose hawkbits hawksbeard hemlock honeysuckle hop trefoil horseradish knapweeds knotgrass mallow meadowsweet melilot mignonette montbretia mullein nettle | nipplewort orchids oxtongue pellitory-of-the- wall pepper saxifrage persicaria poppy privet purple loosestrife ragworts raspberry red bartsia redshank reedmace | restharrow roses scabious scarlet pimpemel sea milkwort sea rocket selflheal sowthistle spearwort St John's worts stonecrops storksbill swinecress thistles thyme-leaved sandwort | common valerian vetches wall lettuce wall rocket water dropwort weld wild carrot wild celery willowherbs wintercress yarrow yellow iris yellowwort |
| **jul** | angelica balsam burdock burnet saxifrage calamint devilsbit scabious | fleabane giant bellflower goldenrod groundsels gum plant harebell heathers | hedge woundwort helleborine hemp agrimony hempnettle lady's bedstraw marjoram | mint mugwort orache saltwort sawwort sea aster sea beet | sneezewort tansy teasel toadflax upright hedge parsley water parsnip | wild basil wood sage |
| **aug** | autumn gentian | ivy | | | | |
| **any month of the year** | chickweed groundsel | daisy hairy bittercress | field speedwell dandelion | deadnettles gorse | pineappleweed shepherds purse | |

The coastline of North Yorkshire extends for more than 60 miles (100km) between precipitous cliffs at Boulby near the Redcar and Cleveland boundary and the dramatic chalk headland of Flamborough. Mostly it faces north east with areas around Staithes, Whitby and Bempton swept by winds from due north. Reaching over 650ft (200m) on Boulby bank the cliffs are amongst the highest along the English coast. Steep, stark and galeswept in places, they are intersected by small inlets (wykes) and wide bays which have enticed Viking invaders, smugglers, fishermen, whalers, mercantile mariners, writers, artists and holiday makers over the centuries. To a dynamic historical legacy add a unique exposure of an epoch in rock formation, a spectacular landscape and a fascinating assembly of plants, enhanced by a hinterland of moorland landscape to the north and wide wolds scenery to the south – no wonder that most of this cliff line is a Heritage Coast. A cliff edge path traverses almost the full extent with tracks to the shore radiating from numerous cliff top car parks and small village settlements; sea level parking is limited to the main resorts – Runswick, Sandsend, Whitby, Scalby, Scarborough and Filey.

North Yorkshire cliffs are formed of sedimentary rocks deposited some 190-135 million years ago. Their complex strata of shales, siltstones, thin limestones and sandstones are interleaved with beds of ironstone, coal, jet and alum shale, and provide a near complete vertical exposure of the Jurassic sequence until at Reighton they sink below the Cretaceous, white, chalk cliffs of Flamborough.

*primroses and scurvygrass carried seawards by slumped boulder clay*

From a botanical standpoint more relevant than the underlying geology is the capping (often many metres deep) of glacial debris deposited at the end of the last ice age some 12,000 years ago, and covering practically all cliff tops and slopes down to the shore. At cliff top it provides a nutrient rich agricultural soil which, especially in post-war decades of profitable farming, was intensively cultivated to within breath-taking proximity of the edge. On cliff slopes plant diversity reflects the mixed origins of boulder clay scraped along by glacial movement. Basically a sticky unstable silt embedded with all manner of weathered rocks and pebbles, it is subject to continuous disintegration from water and frost action. Erosion causes huge chunks to tumble seawards down the cliff face smothering herb-rich swards and producing an assortment of farmland plants among re-colonizing cliff vegetation. Attempts are being made to encourage native plants in some cliff top meadows so that future cliff falls will carry a more indigenous seed resource downslope.

## COASTLINE CHANGES

Ever since medieval times miners and entrepreneurs have exploited the cliffs' resources; alum made (and lost) fortunes for Tudor and later worthies as vast quarries were gouged into the cliffs. Thin seams of coal and ironstone gave rise to elaborate mining schemes with shafts driven perilously into unstable cliffs; a mile-long tunnel and harbour at Port Mulgrave and aerial ropeways elsewhere provided outlets to waiting ships. Jet mining and carving proved a profitable enterprise when Queen Victoria's death popularised black jet jewellery.

The advent of steam trains led to the construction of a scenic rail route with viaducts across ravines, tunnels at Sandsend and Ravenscar, numerous bridges and small stations – all to be abandoned as cliff erosion brought parts of the track ever closer and eventually into the sea. During the railway's heyday holiday resorts expanded and caravan sites increased, further encouraged by road and ribbon development with growing car ownership. It seemed that exploitation might totally destroy the natural beauty of the coast until the Planning Act of 1947 followed by the National Parks and Access to the Countryside Act of 1949 led to formation of the North York Moors National Park in 1952. In 1968 the Countryside Act enabled Heritage Coast designation which effectively limited further adverse development.

Residual effects of this assorted history of human activity can be seen scattered along the coast but plants are great opportunists and where man-made alterations to the land have occurred, a new more appropriate plant community soon builds up. At Runswick Bay, Robin Hood's Bay, Sandsend and Scarborough recent cliff falls have necessitated extensive stabilising works thereby releasing a seed resource previously buried beneath boulder clay. A profusion of orchids including *bee orchid* and many other unusual plants make these some of our most floristic cliffs. The disused railtrack has produced another specialised plant community.

Much cliff land remains unaffected by the hand of man and on these widely varying stretches a diverse natural flora has evolved. Grass species ranging from 2m tall plumes of *tall fescue* to the dainty 3cm *hairgrass* usually form a backdrop to a host of colourful wildflowers. Well over 400 different species or about one fifth of the total British flora have been recorded on the North Yorkshire coast.

Where a plant is growing provides an important clue to its identification as each species has evolved over thousands of years to favour a particular niche in the landscape. You will no more find *moschatel* tucked in amongst algae strewn shore boulders than you will see *marram grass* in Hayburn woods. But some species have a far wider tolerance than others – *creeping bent* appears to be everywhere – while *bithynian vetch* and *bloody cranesbill* can each find only one site to suit them on this coast.

A plant's preferred location or habitat is influenced by many factors such as soil, light, drainage, aspect, altitude, climate and competition from other plants. Habitat size can range from a few centimetres of stone crevice (microhabitat) to miles of sandy shore. And every habitat has a community of plants grading from the highly specialised which will grow nowhere else to the almost universal species which can adapt to living in a variety of conditions.

The question arises as to how plants reached their preferred habitat in the first place. In the wake of retreating glaciers most land surface was bare rock overlain by soils, gravel, stones and boulders known collectively as glacial till. Into this assorted ground, as climatic conditions improved and meltdown expanded, windblown or animal-carried seed was deposited from adjacent areas which had escaped the full impact of ice overlay; a further influx of seeds gradually spread northwards from the southern UK which was not covered by the ice blanket of the last glaciation and from the continent of Europe which until about 6,000 years ago was joined to Britain by a land bridge. Those seeds deposited in favourable ground germinated to form the basis of the indigenous vegetation we have today (the enormous odds against a seed dropping in a suitable growing location explain the prolific seed production evolved by most plants).

But plant populations are never static with some species unable to compete in changing conditions while opportunist newcomers find a suitable niche. Over several millenia natural plant migration has been augmented by successive human settlers whose food, medicinal and garden plants have taken to the wild – *alexanders* was brought by the Romans, *horseradish* by medieval monks,

hoary cress by home-coming soldiers and more recently *montbretia* and other garden varieties have been planted or discarded by clifftop residents. Man's manipulation of the environment whether it be for industry, transport, farming or tourism has a knock-on effect in the composition of the coastal flora which is likely to be further modified as global warming proceeds.

*alexanders at Scarborough Castle*

**sandy shores** accessible for walkers are mainly at Staithes, Runswick, Sandsend, Whitby, Saltwick, Robin Hood's Bay, Hayburn Wyke, Scarborough, Cayton, the wide sweep of Filey Bay southwards to Reighton and small bays on Flamborough headland – covering roughly 18 miles (28km) or less than a third of the total North Yorkshire coast line. Most of these beaches are swept daily by incoming tides so that opportunity for strandline plants to establish is largely confined to cliff indents where streams meander seawards. This can be seen at Hob Holes, Runswick, at Raithwaite, Low Row and Sandsend becks, at Upgang ravine, around Whitby harbour, at Mill beck and Stoupe beck in Robin Hood's Bay, at Hayburn beck, Cloughton and Burniston Wykes and in Filey Bay. At Cayton and Reighton shallow cliff gradients create slightly raised refuges for shore plants. Strandline plants along this coast include:

*orache and sea sandwort on Cayton sands*

| | | |
|---|---|---|
| *sea milkwort* | *marram* | *sea arrowgrass* |
| *sea beet* | *sand couch* | *sea spurreys* |
| *sea sandwort* | *sea rocket* | *lymegrass* |
| *scurvygrass* | *saltmarsh rush* | *saltwort* |

*frosted, spear-leaved, grass-leaved and common oraches*
*sea and stagshorn plantains*

**rocky shores** cover the tidal stretches between sandy bays. Either strewn with boulders or exposing bare rock strata as in Robin Hood's Bay they are twice daily scoured by seawater. Seaweeds spread over these shores, species varying with the extent of tidal inundation. Few flowering plants are able to survive this semi-submerged and turbulent saltwater environment.

*Burniston Wyke*

**saltmarsh** and **mudflats** are poorly represented on this coast where the only tidal river of sufficient size to spread over adjacent grassland is the Esk flowing out through Ruswarp and Whitby. An area known as Ruswarp Batts between these two settlements has tide washed creeks and marsh with:

| | | |
|---|---|---|
| *wild celery* | *hemlock water dropwort* | *sea clubrush* |
| *sea milkwort* | *marsh arrowgrass* | *saltmarsh rush* |
| *scurvygrass* | *false fox sedge* | *common reed* |
| *sea aster* | *sea spurreys* | |

## herb rich grassland occurs

frequently both in small patches on the cliff face and more extensively on the tops where substantial areas of open and recreational ground and fields are sympathetically managed – often under conservation schemes – to retain and improve biodiversity. Less common species may be restricted to specific locations eg *brookweed* at Flamborough and *woolly thistle* at Cayton but much land is colourful throughout the summer with:

| | | |
|---|---|---|
| *common centaury* | *red fescue* | *tansy* |
| *wild carrot* | *devilsbit scabious* | *golden rod* |
| *golden oatgrass* | *salad burnet* | *burnet saxifrage* |
| *hayrattle* | *catsear* | *selfheal* |
| *birdsfoot trefoil* | *clovers* | *eyebright* |
| *field scabious* | *hawkbits* | *fairy flax* |
| *harebell* | *mouse-ear* | *wood sage* |
| *buttercups* | *quaking grass* | *speedwells* |
| *wood, bush and tufted vetches* | | *black medick* |

*orchids – common spotted, pyramidal, northern marsh, early purple, bee, fragrant and twayblade*

## cliff slopes provide a variety of microhabitats dependent on aspect,

gradient, drainage and composition of the boulder clay. Quite recent landslips soon display a selection of:

| | |
|---|---|
| *coltsfoot* | *primrose* |
| *wild carrot* | *scurvygrass* |
| *fleabane* | *kidney vetch* |
| *hayrattle* | *restharrow* |
| *plantains* | *ragworts* |
| *centaury* | *scabious* |
| *hawkbits* | *orchids* |
| *birdsfoot trefoil* | *mayweeds* |
| *meadow vetchling* | |
| *grass of Parnassus* | |

*a colourful slope alongside a shore path in Filey bay*

With the passage of time more permanent scrub may develop with *hawthorn, gorse, blackthorn, bramble, bracken* and *dogrose*, eventually joined by stunted trees to create impenetrable thickets.

## old alum quarries

(Kettleness was the last to close down in 1871) have next to no vegetation on burnt shale debris but as humus starts to accumulate acid heath develops with a limited range of plants such as *bilberry, heather, bell heather, tormentil, heath bedstraw, gorse, catsear, wavy hairgrass, great hairy woodrush* and *ferns*. Marsh plants colonise pockets of water trapped between spoil heaps.

*Deepgrove quarries near Sandsend*

**wetland** on slopes and undercliffs produces a mosaic of open water, marsh and flushes where moisture seeps out above impervious rocks; likely plants here are:

| | | |
|---|---|---|
| *meadowsweet* | *marsh valerian* | *reedmace* |
| *water mint* | *hemp agrimony* | *branched bur-reed* |
| *rushes* | *yellow flag iris* | *clubrushes* |
| *great hairy willowherb* | *arrowgrass* | *glaucous sedge* |
| *horsetails (great, common or marsh)* | | *yellowwort* |
| *watercress* | *ragged robin* | *marsh marigold* |

**rank grassland** is widespread along the cliff top with:

| | |
|---|---|
| *brambles* | *plantains* |
| *tall fescue* | *hogweed* |
| *cocksfoot* | *yarrow* |
| *softgrass* | *elder* |
| *couch grass* | *docks* |
| *sorrel* | *bent grasses* |
| *thistles* | *knapweed* |
| *corn sowthistle* | |
| *false oatgrass* | |
| *rosebay willowherb* | |

Spreading on to tracks and waste ground from adjacent arable fields are occasional annuals such as *scarlet pimpernel, field pansy, field forgetmenot, red deadnettle, field bindweed* and *speedwells*.

**woodlands** may cover large areas as at Runswick and Cornelian Bays or be confined to small ravines where cliffs are incised by streams tumbling seawards eg Oakham wood near Hawsker. Regardless of size nearly all are 'ancient woodland' – a term used to describe deciduous mixed woods on the site of original wildwood; although the tree cover will have been felled, coppiced and replanted, woodland of a sort is likely to have been continuous over centuries. This habitat evolves a specialised diverse ground flora likely to include:

| | | |
|---|---|---|
| ramsons | dogs mercury | ivy |
| primrose | lesser celandine | ground ivy |
| herb robert | wood sorrel | wood anemone |
| red campion | bugle | hairy woodrush |
| bluebell | moschatel | golden saxifrage |
| violets | figwort | early purple orchid |
| wood avens | enchanter's nightshade | goldilocks |
| yellow pimpernel | | |

hartstongue, male, broad buckler and soft shield ferns.

Much rarer are *broad-leaved helleborine* around Fylingthorpe, *lily-of-the-valley* and *spurge laurel* at Runswick and *giant bellflower* at Hayburn Wyke. Tree canopy is usually dominated by sea-tolerant *sycamores* but often includes *ash, hybrid oaks, wych elm, willows (crack, sallow* and *goat), hazel, holly, rowan, hawthorn* and less often *field maple* and *birch,* with *dogrose, elder, gorse, wood vetch* and *honeysuckle* on woodland edges.

**disused railtrack** with free-draining ballast and earthworks provides scope for various dry habitat species. An old rail embankment near Stoupe Brow has the rare *frog orchid* but its survival is in doubt following track drainage which prevents grazing. This gradual scrub encroachment alongside the old coast railway diminishes its floral diversity but many stretches away from woodland continue to produce a variety of plants through the season. Where the original railtrack drainage ditch survives another specialised habitat is colonised by moisture-loving plants including *yellow flag iris, marsh horsetail* and *hemp agrimony.*

*walkers and riders can enjoy a sequence of flowers along the Whitby-Scarborough railtrack*

**buildings** provide further specalised habitats – *wallflowers* on Whitby Abbey ruins and Lythe bank, *salvia* and *calamint* at Scarborough Castle and unusual *ferns* grow with the dainty *ivy-leaved toadflax* on harbour walls.

## WHERE TO LOOK FOR WILD FLOWERS

### BOULBY

A short walk across fields from the mast on Boulby cliff (at just over 200m the highest point on the east coast) provides a panoramic view of the cliffs stretching south-east beyond Staithes, and reveals the proximity of farmed land to the precipitous cliff edge. Disused quarries part way down the cliff are rather inaccessible and have a dense acid heath community of *heath bedstraw, heather, tormentil, bilberry, cottongrass, bell heather* and *gorse* with clumps of *soft rush* and *broad buckler fern*. Exposed to fierce winds in cliff top fields *hoary ragwort* and *common hempnettle* grow at the base of stone walls.

### COWBAR NAB

This massive headland affording shelter to Staithes harbour is gale-swept and difficult to access except by a colony of herring gulls who live amongst the only substantial population on this coast of *slender thistle*. Cowbar Lane is lined with *scurvygrass* and on rocky outcrops prominent blue-green crinkled leaves of *wild cabbage* contrast with shiny green segmented leaves of *wild parsley* and feathery foliage of

*slender thistle on Cowbar Nab with Boulby cliff beyond*

*hemlock*. Long dark green tongue-like leaves of *horse-radish* may be a legacy of days when a peppery sauce was made locally from its grated root. As Cowbar Lane dips steeply towards Staithes Beck its side is clad with *Duke of Argyll's teaplant* whose flowers resemble those of potato or tomato but are a striking purple. The curious name for this shrub is said to arise from a 17th century duke who despatched plant hunters to Asia in search of seedlings with which to establish a tea plantation on his estate. The fate of the unfortunate searchers who returned with the wrong shrub is not recorded!

### STAITHES

Staithes has a limited flora for gale force winds and fierce tides (which in 1953 demolished the harbourside Cod and Lobster Inn) allow only seaweeds to survive on the shore. In a sheltered grassy streamside *common mallow* and *wall barley* grow beside *blackthorn, dogrose, elder, broom* and *hawthorn* scrub. Between Staithes and Port Mulgrave the coastal path divides farmland from windswept grassland where sturdy species such as *sorrel, knapweed, ribwort plantain* and *false oatgrass* are replaced here and there on patches of calcareous ground by *common spotted orchids, weld* and *small scabious*.

## PORT MULGRAVE

A 19th century relic of a once thriving ironstone industry when ore from nearby Grinkle mine was brought by rail through a mile-long tunnel to this small harbour for shipment to Jarrow. The mine closed in 1916, entry to the tunnel was sealed, and the sea is relentlessly demolishing the harbour at the same time as erosion is making a pathway down the cliff increasingly hazardous. Persistent plants in this changing

*disintegrating walls of Port Mulgrave harbour*

environment are *orache, common saltmarsh grass* and *false fox sedge* rooted in saline mud on the disintegrating harbour floor and *blackthorn* with *nettles, bracken* and *rosebay willowherb* on cliff pastures. Whereas former occupants of the small cliff top settlement were involved with harbour work and supplemented income by rearing cattle, today interests lie elsewhere and grazing has all but ceased. This has had a detrimental effect on plant variety with shrub encroachment going on apace and former rarities such as dyers greenweed, yellowwort, greater lettuce, wormwood and wild clary not seen for some years. *Common spotted orchids* and *common centaury* survive on open areas of the crumbling cliff and *wood vetch* scrambles over low scrub. A mix of acid heath and calcareous grassland on Lingrow cliffs produces *heathers, slender St John's wort, quaking grass, weld, primroses* and *bitter vetch.*

## RUNSWICK BAY

The bay has comparatively sheltered waters for sailing and an accessible sandy beach. Although at high water it is covered by the tide to the cliff base, a small stream-cut creek at Hob Holes provides sufficient stability for *sea sandwort* and *frosted orache* to survive. Within the bay a sweeping arc of woodland rises gradually from near shore level to the cliffs some 100m above. Several streams have cut steep narrow ravines

*Runswick Bay*

through the wood thus preventing a feasible path alongside the sands at high water – an alternative pathway along the old railway track from Whitby to Teesside takes a wide curve inland here. It is in this old deciduous woodland that Runswick's botanical richness lies. Amongst common woodland herbs such as *wild arum, wood anemone, sanicle, bluebell, primrose* and *violets* grow bushes of *spurge laurel* and *burnet rose*; carpets of *moschatel* and *lily-of-the-valley*; and vines of *old man's beard* or *traveller's joy* which reaches its most northerly location here. *Wood vetch* scrambles across open shrubby areas. Verges by the cliff to shore road have *restharrow, common toadflax, alexanders* and *tall melilot.*

In 1664 most of the original fishing village of Runswick vanished into the sea with a mighty cliff fall but some cottages remained along with an ancient road from cliff top to shore. When a growing holiday industry brought more affluence, hundreds of *wild cherry* trees were planted on both sides and although the track is today only an eroding footpath, the white flowered cherries show up across the bay as they replace white *blackthorn* blossom of a month before. In common with most coastal settlements various introduced species have become integrated in the local flora. Clumps of bright orange *montbretia* plumes contrast with swathes of white flowered *shasta daisy* and spreading shrubs of dark red *Japanese rose.* A legacy from an earlier type of fodder crop grown in clifftop fields is purple flowered *lucerne,* now established around Runswick Bay Sailing Clubhouse. Shortly before the sands are replaced by a rocky shore beneath near barren vertical cliffs, a path from Hob Holes winding up to High Cliff cuts through lias shales and ironstone strata to sandstone providing habitat for *wild carrot, burnet saxifrage, scarlet pimpernel, hairy St John's wort, autumn gentian, thyme* and *ground ivy.*

## KETTLENESS

A short cliff top walk from Runswick skirts arable fields where *heath, wall* and *common field speedwells, cut-leaved deadnettle, field woundwort, parsley piert* and *dovesfoot cranesbill* can be found. The Ness or headland shows the enormous earth movements carried out by alum, jet and ironstone miners. Upper

parts have vanished leaving a denuded landscape of red burnt shale and grey quarry waste. Patchy scrub vegetation includes *heather* or *ling, bell heather, gorse, great hairy woodrush, bramble, bracken* and *blackthorn.* Grassy areas have a mosaic with *ragwort, goatsbeard, wood sage, lady's bedstraw, carline thistle, red* and *white clovers, harebells* and *smooth hawksbeard. Mugwort* grows with *nettles* and *willowherbs* in rank grassland. East of Kettleness, beyond an old railway embankment where *tansy* and *red bartsia* grow, the cliff towers above Seaveybog, an undercliff with dense *gorse, bracken, blackthorn* and *brambles* surrounding an enclave of wetland plants by a small pond.

Past Keldhowe the cliff path plunges into Overdale, a relic of ancient woodland with *oak, ash, holly, sycamore, hazel, hawthorn, rose* and numerous *wych elm* outnumbering a few planted *beech, Scots pine* and *rhododendron.* Tall plants of *greater bellflower* and *pendulous sedge* arise from a carpet of *bluebell, harts-tongue fern, wood sorrel, golden saxifrage, dogs mercury, herb robert, early purple orchids, red campion* and *violets.* Fungi flourish on fallen decaying timber. Cliff tops have a grassland community with *common knapweed, ribwort* and *sea plantains, lady's bedstraw, wood sage* and *devilsbit scabious* scattered between sturdy grasses such as *cocksfoot* and *tall oatgrass.* On field edges *ramping fumitory i*s quite widespread and the rare *shepherd's needle* appears from time to time.

## SANDSEND

At the northern end of the bay where three centuries ago Sandsend Ness would have been a formidable headland, Deepgrove alum extraction has created a unique landscape. Plants thriving on free-draining acidic quarry waste include *bell heather, gorse* and the tiny *early* and *silver hairgrasses* and *golden oatgrass* but widespread hollows have trapped water and debris sufficient for a rich plant community. Here are stands of *yellow flag iris, hemp agrimony, great* and *water horsetails, marsh pennywort, fleabane* and *meadowsweet* with colonies of *common spotted* and *northern marsh orchids* and a complex range of hybrids.

The disused railway track between Sandsend old station and the sealed tunnel entrance at Deepgrove is home to a mixture of native and introduced plants, the most spectacular being a long established and colourful garden

*wood vertch is common beside the old railtrack*

escape *broad-leaved everlasting-pea* which scrambles extensively over taller plants in the vicinity of the sealed tunnel. Another abundant and more widespread scrambler is the native *wood vetch.* Woodlands maturing west of the track include *sycamore, rowan, gorse, hybrid willows* and *oaks, blackthorn* and *wild rose* with *figwort, lady fern* and *horsetails* dominating the ground flora. Towards the station introductions such as *red valerian, Japanese rose, montbretia* and *wallflower* grow alongside *common mallow* and *alexanders.*

Inlets where three streams meander from the hills to reach the sea together with low sandy cliffs sea-sprayed only at really high tides provide enough stability for a few saline plants to establish. *Sea rocket* appears amidst *frosted* and *common orache, lesser sea-spurrey* and *field bindweed.* Tall spikes of *lymegrass, sand couch, marram* and *sea clubrush* contrast with short spikes of *sea hardgrass* and *sea plantain.* On rough grassland near the road – mostly remains of the former coast railway – grow *hoary* and *Oxford ragworts, wall barley, white stonecrop* and *bittersweet* with patches of mauve *garden aster.* Sandy ground attracts *thyme-leaved sandwort, sea* and *little mouse-ear* in carpets of *stagshorn plantain.*

Towards the end of the 20th century a

*lymegrass dominates a part of Sandsend beach*

major landslide across the Sandsend to Whitby road was followed by radical cliff re-alignment. Newly exposed boulder clay and introduced hardcore now sustain a rich flora including *bee orchid, common centaury, wild carrot, burnet saxifrage, carline thistle, fragrant* and *pyramidal orchids.* In 2003 another landslip nearby spread across the road necessitating further earthworks. At the time of writing this area is bare – it will be interesting to record its gradual re-vegetation. *Hoary cress* and *winter heliotrope* (both incomers to the British flora) fringe a lay-by at the top of the hill approaching Whitby.

## UPGANG RAVINE

The only recorded north of England site for *bithynian vetch,* which grows in grassy scrub on the Sandsend side of the ravine. This plant-rich area has

*bithynian vetch*

*sawwort, devil's bit scabious, fragrant orchid, pepper saxifrage, marjoram* and *restharrow.* Following radical shore defence work in

*Upgang ravine separates Sandsend from Whitby*

the 1990s cliffs sloping away from a new promenade on the Whitby side of the ravine as yet show minimal botanical interest except for a level strip near the sea wall which has *ferngrass, quaking grass, swinecress, birdsfoot trefoil* and *salad burnet.*

## WHITBY

Where the strangely named Khyber Pass curves down to the western pier, the rock face has a unique flora comprised of *wild cabbage, Oxford ragwort, red valerian* and *coastal gumplant* – a North American species well established here in its only known British location. Sea-sprayed walls around the harbour have clusters of *maidenhair spleenwort, wall rue, ivy-leaved toadflax* and *common saltmarsh-grass.* On waste sandy ground below

*Whitby Harbour*

the Abbey headland *eastern rocket* and *sea rocket* appear erratically; and almost every stone wall in this vicinity is clothed with *pellitory-of-the-wall. Hairy tare* fringes the steps leading from harbourside to the Abbey, and *wallflower* grows from ancient stonework within the Abbey precincts. Ongoing structural works to stabilise cliffs and expand the marina leave few habitats accessible for plants but remnants of saltmarsh survive where Spital beck joins the River Esk.

## RUSWARP

The River Esk which flows into the sea at Whitby having drained Eskdale and adjacent valleys is tidal up to Ruswarp where open ground provides the only significant mudflat and saltmarsh along this coast. By no means extensive, these habitats are constricted by harbour development but small patches remain with both *greater* and *lesser sea spurrey, sea aster, saltmarsh rush, sea milkwort, sea arrowgrass* and *sea*

*saltmarsh beside the River Esk at Ruswarp*

*plantain.* Ruswarp Batts has tidal creeks where *hemlock water-dropwort, sea clubrush, distant sedge* and *false fox sedge* survive cattle grazing. *Smooth tare* grows in rough ground close to a large spread of *common reed* in a saline marsh and on old buildings close by the river *annual wall rocket* and *wild celery* can be seen.

Only a few trains run into Whitby station these days with the result that the railtrack, now reduced to a single line, has unsprayed dry ballast areas enjoyed by such plants as *thyme-leaved sandwort, scarlet pimpernel, fumitory, soft brome, corn salad, mouse-eared hawkweed, thalecress, ratstail fescue* and *hairgrasses.*

## SALTWICK

A coastal path east from Whitby demonstrates the never-ending erosion on these friable cliffs where almost every year parts of the path have to be moved further inland. Coarse grassland with *red fescue, hogweed, coltsfoot, cocksfoot, tall fescue* and *false oatgrass* merges into a sward with *pignut, kidney vetch, yarrow, scurvygrass* and *common vetch.* Saltwick Nab is a stark reminder of alum extraction which went on here for over 200 years before finishing around 1860. A promontory of bare shaly residue contrasts with a green undercliff where locally rare *dyer's greenweed* flowers alongside *crowberry* and *bell heather.* Another local rarity *water whorlgrass* inhabits a small stream with *lesser spearwort, common reed, flotegrass, rushes* and *common horsetail.* South of the Nab the sandy shore of Saltwick Bay is reached by a good path from the caravan site above. *Restharrow,* both pink and white flowered, skirts the track with *meadow vetchling, bell heather, hayrattle, golden rod* and *birdsfoot trefoil.* Stands of *marram, sand* and *common couch* grow close to the shore; on the shallow sloping cliff *grass of Parnassus* appears with *common centaury* in seepage ground and *fairy flax, wild carrot* and *cat's-ear* on drier soil.

*burnt alum shale on remains of Saltwick headland*

## HAWSKER

Between Saltwick and Robin Hood's Bay some 6 km of sheer vertical cliff prevent access to the rocky tide-swept shore beneath. Wind-sculpted *blackthorn, gorse, wild rose* and *sycamore* alongside coarse grassland dotted with *primrose, coltsfoot* and *scurvygrass* fringe arable and pasture fields, interrupted at the old lighthouse where *thrift* and *sea buckthorn* cling to rocky outcrops. Near Hawsker Bottoms small streams are lined with *grey willow,*

*many cliffs are ablaze with gorse in springtime*

*hemp agrimony, meadowsweet* and *common reed* and in wooded gulleys ground herbs include *wild arum, wood anemone, ramsoms, red campion, raspberry, golden saxifrage, violets* and *moschatel.* Cliff slopes have drifts of *grass of Parnassus* with *wild carrot, scurvygrass, devilsbit scabious, tufted vetch* and *red clover.*

## ROBIN HOOD'S BAY

Slippage of unstable boulder clay over centuries has caused buildings in this old fishing village to collapse into the sea. To protect remaining dwellings a robust sea wall was built in 1975 and extended more than 20 years later when substantial regrading of the cliff took place. This led to the appearance – possibly only for a few years – of unusual plant species inlcuding *white and tall melilot, prickly oxtongue, gallant soldier* and *chicory.* Marshy ground in Marnardale, a narrow wooded valley south of the slipway, has *ragged robin, marsh marigold* and *water mint* mingled with *lesser celandine, soft* and *hard rushes, goldilocks buttercup* and *ivy-leaved crowfoot.*

In the sweep of the bay, slopes resulting from cliff subsidence provide roothold for *early purple orchid, restharrow, coltsfoot, white campion, bluebell, primrose* and *common spotted orchid.*

Ancient woodland fills the valleys of Stoupe beck and Mill beck (where Boggle Hole youth hostel occupies the old mill). Ferns abound here, particularly *hartstongue, male fern, broad buckler, lady fern, polypody* and *hard shield* under a canopy of *wych elm, hazel, sycamore, alder* and *ash.*

The track between Stoupe beck and Ravenscar skirts heather moorland, one of the few places where this habitat lies close to the sea.

*bell heather fringes cliff-top fields in Robin Hood's Bay*

## RAVENSCAR

A sandy shore continues halfway to Ravenscar until replaced by seaweed-covered boulders and rocks up to the tide-lashed base of tall bare cliffs where only a few clumps of *scurvygrass* survive. Land rises from Stoupe beck to a sweep of heather moorland with *bilberry, crowberry, ling, heath orchids* and *cottongrass*. The track of the former Scarborough to Whitby railway

*rowan trees abound on Ravenscar hillsides*

together with vast alum quarries, their workyards and an old brickworks indicate the scale of industrial activity here in days gone by. Today there is minimal interference with a variety of common species such as *knapweed, nipplewort, speedwells, vetches, bulbous buttercup, meadow vetchling, creeping cinquefoil, harebells* and *foxglove* – and a few local rarities – *frog orchid, rockrose, adderstongue* and *moonwort*. An unwelcome newcomer is *Himalayan balsam* rampaging through scrubland to the detriment of native species. *Primroses* are plentiful but *cowslip* is scarcely seen here. *Reedmace, willows, wild angelica, broad-leaved pondweed* and *golden saxifrage* have colonised wet areas where *butterwort, round-leaved sundew, marsh valerian, large bittercress, marsh violet, common centaury, ragged robin* and *greater birdsfoot trefoil* grow. On dry ground, especially amongst old shale heaps, *climbing corydalis, wood sage* and *broom* are plentiful. Alum quarrying took place a field or two back from the cliff edge and has left gaping hollows in the hillside, now home to *rowan, gorse, bilberry, oval sedge, heather* and *bell heather*. Around the village of Ravenscar planted hedges of *oleria* survive the salt-laden winds but nature's protective shield is *blackthorn* which dominates the cliff edge.

South from the headland of Old Peak centuries old subsidence has left a series of undercliffs, now largely covered with mature wood or scrub and difficult of access. Open glades and varied rock strata are colonised by a range of plant species including *wood* and *bitter vetch, carline thistle, honeysuckle, fragrant* and *dog violets, bluebells, primroses* (including many pink petalled), *common spotted, fragrant, pyramidal* and *early purple orchids, barren strawberry* and *thyme.*

*windswept Ravenscar on its lofty headland*

### HAYBURN WYKE

Deep In ancient woodland on hillsides sloping towards Hayburn beck is secreted the rare *hay-scented buckler fern*, but easier to see are *wood anemones, bugle, wood avens, black bryony, great woodrush, wild arum* and *ground ivy* beneath a mixed canopy of *ash, oak, rowan, alder, birch, holly, hazel* and planted conifers. Where the beck spreads into the sea clumps of *common couch, sea beet* and *orache* grow between rocks on the tide-line. Scattered plants of *grass of Parnassus* and *common centaury* cling to the salt-sprayed cliffs along with *sea spleenwort*. This small fern also occurs a short distance south at Roger Trod, its most southerly site on the east coast of Britain. Although 100m high cliffs hereabouts plummet steeply seawards, ledges retain a grassy sward rich with *golden rod, devilsbit scabious* and occasional *fragrant orchids* amongst *harebells, common knapweed* and *burnet saxifrage.*

### CLOUGHTON

Where the cliff path slopes towards Cloughton Wyke it crosses Sycarham wood. Shelter from wind and sea-spray given by salt-resistant *sycamores,* combined with a southern aspect, encourage a diverse ground flora including *wild daffodil* – a plant rarely seen on the coastal fringe. These delicate flowers contrast with clumps of larger garden narcissi planted round about.

*wild daffodils carpet the floor of Sycarham wood*

Indicating this wood's ancient origin are *toothwort, wild garlic, wood anemone, bluebell, wood sorrel, wild arum* and abundant *climbing corydalis* along with *red campion, wood sage* and *ground ivy. Common reed* extends to shore level at **Burniston Wyke** further south.

### SCALBY

Flood waters from a channel cut to link with the River Derwent have enlarged Scalby beck and created a shallow small clay-filled valley behind cliffs at Scalby Ness. Despite frequent inundation, *yellowwort* and *grass of Parnassus* flourish here. Occasional stands of *water plantain, large bittercress, common reed, fleabane, hemp agrimony* and *wild angelica* reveal constant moisture but adjacent well-drained slopes have a varied grassland flora with *orchids, goatsbeard, salad* and *greater burnet, hairy sedge, agrimony, tufted vetch, common hempnettle, autumn* and *hairy hawkbits, wild carrot* and *lady's bedstraw. Wood vetch* scrambles amongst *dog rose, gorse* and *brambles* while *bristly oxtongue* appears erratically on waste ground around the carpark.

## SCARBOROUGH NORTH BAY

Because the north bay between Scalby and Scarborough Castle provides a sandy beach and easy access, it has been well developed for recreation despite the proximity of clay cliffs. Towards the end of the 20th century serious erosion necessitated extensive engineering to protect the

*flower rich slope near Scarborough north bay seafront*

resort. The outcome botanically has been to produce an array of *orchids – (pyramidal, common spotted, bee* and *fragrant) –* amidst *tall melilot, mignonette, hayrattle, kidney vetch, zig-zag* and *white clovers, creeping cinquefoil, meadow vetchling, smooth hawksbeard, ramping fumitory, common centaury, eyebright* and *crosswort –* all just a stone's throw from the miniature railway and footpath. A semi-wild grassy promenade is home to *mouse-ear hawkweed, black medick, fairy flax, sand couch, lymegrass, marram, golden oatgrass* and *reflexed saltmarsh grass* with abundant *sea mayweed* and *stagshorn plantain.*

## SCARBOROUGH CASTLE

Unlike the previous species-rich site resulting from recent disturbance, Scarborough Castle headland owes its unusual plant community to a series of weather resistant rock strata capped with corallian limestone. Beneath the ramparts grow *wild clary, spotted medick* and *common calamint*, all plants scarcely known elsewhere in north-east Yorkshire. On the ancient walls are *wallflower, ferngrass, hartstongue fern, red valerian, white stonecrop* and *pellitory-of-the-wall* while base-rich slopes around the castle ramparts are colourful with *marjoram, weld, mallow, black horehound, field mouse-ear, dropwort* and *sea beet*. Inside the castle precincts grassland is managed to enhance a herb-rich sward with *orchids, hayrattle, hoary plantain, birdsfoot trefoil, knapweed, clovers* and *vetches*.

## SCARBOROUGH SOUTH BAY

In 1995 a massive landslide on Scarborough south cliff took Holbeck Hall Hotel into the sea, leaving a gaping chasm to be stabilised with imported boulders and hardcore. This created a new plant habitat which soon attracted *pyramidal orchid, common spotted orchid, kidney vetch* and *centaury. Winter heliotrope*, an opportunist garden plant spreading throughout Britain, is well established along with *coltsfoot, ox-eye daisy, red* and *white clovers, fleabane, restharrow* and *birdsfoot trefoil*.

### CORNELIAN BAY

A footpath to the shore from a residential area on the outskirts of Scarborough cuts through thickly wooded ferny cliff slopes with *sycamore, blackthorn, hawthorn, hazel, wild privet* and *willows.* Subsidence is taking large shrubs of *sea buckthorn* seawards from a landscaped golf course above. Water seepage through boulder clay has formed several lime-rich flushes along these cliffs, providing ideal habitat for *grass of Parnassus, glaucous sedge, coltsfoot, fleabane* and *primrose.* On drier areas *early purple orchids* and *cowslips* are followed by *carline thistle, small scabious, bee orchids, hoary ragwort* and *wild carrot. Woolly thistle* grows on an exposed headland at Osgodby (or Knipe) point, its only known site on this coast.

### CAYTON BAY

Cliffs encircling this broad sandy shore have a modest gradient where spring seepage into mixed grassland, woodland and wetland creates exceptionally flower-rich slopes. At the cliff foot are small areas with strandline vegetation – *sea rocket, sea sandwort, frosted* and *spear-leaved orache.* Rock falls at the northern end of the bay enclose a small shore level pond where stands of tall *sea* and *common clubrush, common reed* and

*kidney vetch spreads from cliff top to shore at Cayton Bay*

*reedmace* overtop *purple loosestrife, arrowgrass, branched bur-reed* and *celery-leaved buttercup. False fox sedge* grows nearby. Higher up on Tenants Cliff fresh-water marshes have *flote-grass, water crowfoot, water forgetmenot, pondweed, yellow flag iris* and *bittersweet.* Locally rare are *dropwort* flowers in the surrounding herb-rich meadow and *spring beauty* near a sandy path.

### GRISTHORPE CLIFFS

Dividing Cayton bay from Gristhorpe cliff is the headland of Yons Nab where *grass of Parnassus* proliferates on precipitous slumps of boulder clay. A coast path skirts fields which are cultivated close to the edge but several caravan sites occupy the cliff top where land is managed either to maintain open space for recreation or for wildlife conservation. Several colourful meadows have a succession of *field buttercup, birdsfoot trefoil, white clover, catsear, knapweed, hawkbits, bladder campion* and *eyebright.* Alongside the cliff path look out for *bee* and *common spotted orchids* and *goatsbeard* as well as a local rarity – *pepper saxifrage.* Bourne Leisure Parks, the National Trust and Filey Brigg Ornithological Group are some of the landowners managing fields to retain, improve and, wherever possible, extend species-rich cliff top grassland further inland to compensate for the never-ending loss of land at the cliff edge. These conservation schemes are important both to retain wildflower diversity on the tops and to provide a range of native seeds to colonise newly eroded cliff slopes.

## FILEY BRIGG

Filey Brigg has long been a mecca for birdwatchers observing seasonal migration. Cliff top pools have been created to assist migrant birds and expand this natural bird observatory. Plants soon colonised with marshy ground around the pools making ideal habitat for *saltmarsh rush, water crowfoot, sea milkwort,*

*yellow flag iris, hard rush, sea arrowgrass, reed canary grass* and *spike rush.* Well-trodden ground nearby is spread with *stagshorn plantain, swinecress, scurvygrass* and *sea plantain.* In adjacent coarse grassland *perennial sowthistle* is prolific accompanied by *hoary ragwort, kidney vetch, sea mayweed* and *welted thistle.* Rank grassland on Carr Nase contrasts with pockets of lime-loving plants on cliff ledges.

## PRIMROSE VALLEY and HUNMANBY

South of Filey town more stable, tiered cliffs have a scrub vegetation enriched by calcareous soils and largely free from wave action. This popular sandy beach, accessed by thousands of visitors from the large Primrose Valley holiday village above, has some of the most colourful cliffs on the coast. In grassland only a metre back from the beach can be seen brilliant magenta flowers of *bloody cranesbill* with *kidney vetch, coltsfoot, primrose, twayblade, wild carrot, betony* and *sawwort.* On dry areas *quaking grass, milkwort* and *carline thistles*

*bloody cranesbill at Primrose Valley*

contrast with *yellowwort, centaury* and *orchids* (especially *bee); unusually deep purple colouration of *pyramidal orchids* may reflect a high nutrient boulder clay in this vicinity. *Burnet rose* grows amidst *hawthorn, bramble* and *blackthorn* scrub, also a rarity on this coast – *rockrose.* Both *arrowgrasses* are plentiful on flushes.

Presumably escaped from the many caravan and bungalow gardens on the cliff top, several garden species flowering alongside native wildflowers include *montbretia, shasta daisy, snow-in-summer, weigelia, yellow loosestrife, Japanese knotweed, fuchsia, teasel, lupin, bridewort* and *cotoneaster.* A landscape once managed as part of a holiday camp has opportunist species such as *mugwort, foxglove* and *scarlet pimpernel* on rabbit-grazed wasteland and moisture-loving *hemp agrimony, false fox sedge* and *bottle sedge, water plantain, ragged robin, celery-leaved buttercup, bistort, marsh valerian* and *tubular water dropwort* have colonised a former boating lake, now coated with locally rare *ivy-leaved duckweed.*

### REIGHTON

Buffeting tides prevent sustainable plant cover at shore level, but cliffs here slope back to a long-established, sandy, raised beach on which *dovesfoot cranesbill, scarlet pimpernel, eyebright, ferngrass, carline thistle, violets, centaury, common* and *sticky mouse-ear,*

*Bempton and Flamborough cliffs from Reighton*

*creeping cinquefoil, lesser, hairy* and *autumn hawkbits, mouse-ear hawkweed, restharrow, stagshorn* and *sea plantains* flourish. A rough track to the beach from a small carpark higher up crosses this unusual free-draining stretch of level undercliff. Elsewhere scrub has developed with *gorse, bramble, elder, dogrose* (some clumps of *Japanese rose), sycamore, blackthorn* and *hawthorn* entwined with *large bindweed* and *rosebay willowherb.* On grassy open areas are *hoary ragwort, coltsfoot, common spotted* and *early purple orchids, meadow vetchling, harebell, teasel, catsear, smooth hawksbeard* and *fleabane.* A broad hollow gouged by landslip and stream action retains a watery base ideal for *branched bur-reed, reedmace, common reed* and a community of *ferns, sedges, orchids* and wetland plants in an impenetrable *willow* scrub.

### SPEETON and BUCKTON

Woodland covers the lower part of a small valley cut by Reighton beck on its way to the sea. Mainly *sycamore*, once the leaf canopy closes over the spring ground flora, ferns dominate but look out for *tutsan,* a relic of ancient woodland. On a wide undercliff a wet and dry mosaic has attracted *meadowsweet, twayblade, silverweed, herb robert, kidney vetch, lady's mantle* and *wild angelica.* Primroses, *kidney vetch* and *coltsfoot* are widespread, followed later in the year by *fragrant, pyramidal, northern marsh* and *common spotted orchids.* Until gentle grassy cliff slopes merge into steep stony scree they provide habitat for *small scabious* and

*pyramidal orchid with restharrow on Speeton cliffs*

*burnet saxifrage* as well as a range of common species including *cow parsley, upright hedge parsley, bush vetch, tormentil, germander speedwell, ragwort, harebell* and *lady's bedstraw.*

As the broad sweep of Filey bay gives way to the sheer cliffs of Flamborough headland, so the Jurassic sequence sinks beneath Cretaceous chalks, albeit still largely capped with glacial till.

## BEMPTON

These steep vertical cliffs, home to thousands of sea birds, are coated with guano which sustains a profusion of *red campion*. *Hemlock* grows alongside the cliff top path with *burdock, yarrow, curled* and *broad-leaved docks, white deadnettle, greater stitchwort* and *sorrel*. *Ribwort plantain* and *bulbous buttercup* are frequent in adjacent fields.

*red campion on Bempton cliffs*

## FLAMBOROUGH

Short turf with *bent* and *fescue grasses*, *hoary, sea* and *stagshorn plantains, sea mayweed, scurvygrass, sea arrowgrass* and *saltmarsh grass* forms the basic ground cover surrounding the many coves and bays eroded into this chalk headland – liberally sprinkled with groups of *primrose, violets, bluebells, thrift , glaucous sedge, coltsfoot, quaking grass, vetches, medicks* and *clovers*. But every stride reveals species indicating subtle habitat variations. Swathes of *northern marsh orchids* spread across grassland in Thornwick Bay; a nearby rivulet has *marsh marigold* and other wetland plants; *weld, salad burnet, wild carrot, kidney vetch, common centaury, storksbill, catsear* and *hayrattle* are scattered around the headland; *alexanders* appears mainly in Selwicks Bay; *thrift* is plentiful on grassy areas near the lighthouse with *wild carrot* and *salad burnet*; a nearby marsh has *butterwort, ragged robin, tall melilot, yellowwort* and *grass of Parnassus.* A wet gully south of the lighthouse has a large population of *brookweed*. Harebells, *pyramidal* and *common spotted orchids* grow with *restharrow* at North Landing.

On cliff tops *greater* and *common knapweed* are frequent along with *lady's bedstraw, scabious, agrimony, bulbous buttercup* and *birdsfoot trefoil*. Pink trumpeted *field bindweed* carpets the ground in places.

*thrift and catsear on Flamborough cliffs*

31

### 2-4 petals

**COMMON SCURVYGRASS** *Cochlearia officinalis*
Is practically confined to the coast; frequent on gale swept cliffs and seashores above the strandline; fleshy shining

leaves and small short-stemmed white flowers on low plants; not a grass despite the name; with a high vitamin C content it was an essential part of early seafarers' diets to prevent scurvy. Apr-Aug.

**DANISH SCURVYGRASS**
*Cochlearia danica*
Is smaller than common scurvygrass; pinkish petals and ivy-shaped leaves on a compact ground-hugging plant; widespread inland on the splash zone of salted roads but rare on this coast; winter annual. Feb-May.

**GARLIC MUSTARD** *Alliaria petiolata*
Common robust wayside plant in flower from April onwards; light green thin leaves smell of garlic if broken; varies from 20 -120cm tall; a country-wide plant with many local names such as hedge garlic and Jack-by-the-hedge.

**HOARY CRESS** *Lepidium draba*
Accidentally introduced in straw mattresses by soldiers returning to Wales in 1802, this plant has spread to road verges at Sands-end, Whitby and Scarborough; grey green leaves clasp 30cm stems with bunches of short stalked small flowers; grows in dense colonies. May-Aug

**ENCHANTERS NIGHTSHADE**
*Circaea lutetiana*
A shade-loving plant of moist deciduous woods along the cliffs eg Cayton, Stoupe Beck; slender stems 20-60cm tall have tiny single-stalked flowers – their 2 notched petals may appear as 4; pointed oval leaves lower down. Jun-Aug.

**HORSERADISH** *Armoracia rusticana*
Frequent around Staithes and Whitby often on road verges; flower bunches grow above clumps of long shiny tongue-like leaves; the root is ground to make a peppery sauce traditionally served with roast beef.
Jun-Jul.

Farmland weeds such as wild radish, pennycress and fools parsley occasionally spread to the cliffs from nearby fields.

**WATERCRESS** *Rorippa nasturtium-aquaticum* Familiar salad plant with winter-green roundish leaflets, hollow fleshy stems; sprawls in shallow slow streams; flowers in clusters. May-Oct.

**LARGE BITTERCRESS** *Cardamine amara* Grows in a few shady pools to the north; erect stems to 60cm have dark green foliage and white flowers up to 1cm across with conspicuous <u>violet</u> anthers. Apr-Jun.

**SHEPHERDS PURSE** *Capsella bursa-pastoris* Widespread on disturbed ground; variable in size and leaf shape; usually has ground rosette of lobed leaves; small flowers produced all year; cordate seeds are shaped like food pouches carried by shepherds in times past.

**BITTERCRESS** *Cardamine spp.* Named from the tangy flavour of edible leaves; h**airy bittercress** *C. hirsuta* (though hairs may be obscure) makes a neat leafy ground rosette from which <u>straight</u> flowering stems to 10cm emerge almost all year round; small flower has <u>4 stamens</u>; seeds widely scattered as ripe linear pods 'explode'; a prolific weed of garden and disturbed ground. **Wavy bittercress** *C. flexuosa* is taller and prefers a damp shady streamside; has <u>zig-zag stems</u> to 50cm and small flowers with <u>6 stamens</u>.

**THALECRESS** *Arabidopsis thaliana* Rail ballast between Ruswarp and Whitby provides the dry bare habitat required by this winter-germinating annual; leafy ground rosette; small flower clusters on short stems; narrow pods on stalks at right angles to the stem. Apr-May.

**WHITLOWGRASS** *Erophila verna* A diminuitive annual which appears in early spring then withers away by midsummer; can be prolific on dry bare ground where its many tiny flowers on very short stems suggest a light covering of snow.

**SWINECRESS** *Coronopus squamatus* A ground-hugging plant easily overlooked with tiny white flowers hidden in small mats of dull green short leaves; occasional on trampled path and gateways – Filey Carr Nase, Port Mulgrave harbour.

**HOLLY** *Ilex aquifolium*
Evergreen spiny-leaved tree frequent in copse, scrub and hedgerow; the familiar red berries develop from small 4 petalled flowers on female trees; male flowers grow on separate trees. May-Sep.

**WILD PRIVET** *Ligustrum vulgare*
In thick scrub woodland on Cornelian Bay under-cliff, rare elsewhere along the coast; leaves are ± evergreen, elongated oval, narrower than the rounded oval of garden privet; small flowers on short spikes Jun-Jul followed by shiny black berries.

---

# bedstraws
*Galium spp.* have square stems, linear leaflets in whorls, small flowers with 4 (or 5) petals in loose clusters. The name derives from the honey-scented yellow lady's bedtraw once used as a mattress filling.

**HEATH BEDSTRAW** *G.saxatile*
Frequent on moor edge eg Stoupe Brow and in acid soils to the north; low mat-forming plant; hairless smooth lax stems have whorls of 6-8 leaflets and clusters of small white flowers; often with heather and tormentil. Jun-Aug.

**MARSH BEDSTRAW** *G.palustre*
Common in marshy grassland, in pools and cliff flushes where its long stems penetrate dense vegetation; whorls have 4-6 blunt or slightly pointed leaflets. Jun-Aug.

**FEN BEDSTRAW**
*G.uliginosum* Uncommon in calcareous wetland; whorls have 6-8 leaflets each with a small sharp point (mucronate); tiny flowers. Jun-Aug.

---

**WOODRUFF** *Galium odoratum*
An indicator of ancient woodland, plentiful in moist shade at Hawsker, Robin Hood's Bay and Runswick; can cover wide patches; square stems up to 30cm have whorls of 6-8 linear pointed leaflets; at the top are flat sprays of small 4 petalled flowers May-Jun. Strong 'haytime' fragrance from dried plants which were spread on floors in Tudors times as a room freshener.

**CLEAVERS** *Galium aparine*
Myriads of hooked hairs enable 'goosegrass' or 'sticky willy' to clamber extensively in scrub vegetation on cliff tops and slopes; square stems and whorls of 6-8 linear leaflets all edged with prickles; insignificant 4 petalled flowers; bristly small round fruits cling to passers-by. May-Aug.

**BLACKTHORN**
*Prunus spinosa*
On the bleakest cliffs blackthorn defies gale force winds by growing horizontally eg Blea Wyke and Muston. In March small white flowers contrast with dark spiny branches well before bright green

oval toothed leaves appear; blue/ black berries (sloes) later; thickets are widespread except on Flamborough headland.

**GUELDER ROSE** *Viburnum opulus*
This large leafy shrub is not a rose but in the honeysuckle family; infrequent on wood edge; broad flowerheads Jun-Jul are followed by luscious-looking but very poisonous red berries; large lobed leaves.

**WILD CHERRY** *Prunus avium*
Occasional in wooded valleys; various cultivars in villages especially Runswick; flowers cup-shaped with 5 petals and reflexed sepals; oval double-toothed leaves have long stalks and 2 red pimples or glands where blade joins stalk. May-Jun.

**HAWTHORN**
*Crataegus monogyna*
Common shrub on most cliff tops and undercliffs in hedges and scrub woodland; spiny angular branches have sprays of aromatic flowers May-Jun; these mature into the red

berry 'haws' of autumn soon devoured by birds in wintry weather; young foliage said to taste of bread and cheese.

**ELDER** *Sambucus nigra*
A much-branched large shrub frequent in scrub; flat-topped sprays of small creamy flowers mature into bunches of juicy black berries; both are gathered for home wine making; large toothed deciduous leaflets.

**CRAB APPLE** *Malus sylvestris*
Hedgerow tree infrequent along the coast; petals pink tinted; leaves oval pointed, tooth-edged; May-Jun. Small yellowish apples rather hard and sour linger on the tree until winter frosts. An originator of many orchard cultivars.

**BRAMBLE** *Rubus fruticosus*
Prolific on the cliffs where it often forms dense prickly thickets; in May-Aug flowers up to 4cm across range from white to pink; leaf shape and size vary; a vigorous and fast-spreading plant which can engulf nearby vegetaion; succulent black autumn fruits are gathered for home baking – and by migrating birds.

**RASPBERRY** *Rubus idaeus*
Occasional on sunny cliff ledges and in cliff top copses; spreads by root suckers which send up 1m tall prickly stems; petals soon fall from small white flowers in June; familiar tasty red fruits ripe by midsummer; green leaves are downy white beneath.

**BURNET ROSE** *Rosa pimpinellifolia*
This white-flowered rose is infrequent in scrub on cliffs at Runswick, Whitby and Primrose Valley to Reighton; long and short spines dense on bronze stems; spreads by suckers; leaves with 3-5 pairs of neatly toothed leaflets; flowers May-Jul. The only UK wild rose to have black hips instead of red.

**ROWAN** *Sorbus aucuparia*
Occasional on more acidic ground north of Roger Trod; frequent around Ravenscar in hedgerow and scrub; large sprays of small creamy white flowers in May are followed by bunches of red berries; smooth greyish bark; leaves have 5-8 pairs of oval, evenly toothed, leaflets.

**CORN SPURREY** *Spergula arvensis*
Annual of acid arable land formerly grown to provide edible meal for humans and livestock; today regarded as a tiresome weed; spindly stems to 30cm with numerous starry flowers and untidy whorls of narrow leaves; occasional on bare ground and cultivated cliff edge fields eg Cloughton Wyke.

**FAIRY FLAX** *Linum catharticum*
Lax plant frequent on meadows and cliff slopes; slender stems 5-25cm carry starry flowers and pairs of blunt, small leaves May-Sep. The botanical name indicates its stringent qualities, reputedly so severe that it is no longer in medicinal use; its former name of purging flax has been rejected as inappropriate for these elegant small flowers.

**WHITE BRYONY** *Bryonia dioica*
Beyond its normal south-eastern range, a few plants survive in sheltered woodland in Runswick Bay. It scrambles around with coiled tendrils; separate male and female flowers with 5 creamy petals in axils of rough lobed leaves; May-Sep.

**SEA SANDWORT** *Honckenya peploides*
Succulent plant growing in UK only on the maritime fringe; withstands winds, spray and occasional high tides; sprawls extensively on upper shores at Cayton, Sandsend and Runswick; mats of glossy yellow/green leaves on fleshy stems; flowers May-Jun.

**BLINKS**
*Montia fontana*
Creeping plant quite frequent in damp grassland; mat-forming tiny spoon-shaped leaves; flowers only 2-3mm across appear all summer.

**THYME-LEAVED SANDWORT**
*Arenaria serpyllifolia* Frequent on sandy or dry calcareous soils; low creeping annual; hairy oval leaves; flowers 5-6mm, white petals shorter than green sepals. Jun-Aug.

**SPRING BEAUTY**
*Claytonia perfoliata*
Locally rare short annual grows on Tenants cliff, Cayton; tiny white flowers encircled by glossy leaf Apr-May.

**WATER CROWFOOT** *Ranunculus spp.*
Common, pond, thread-leaved and ivy-leaved water crowfoots occur in various ponds and muddy margins eg Cayton shore, near Ravenscar golf course and Filey Carr Nase; all flowers have 5 white petals and yellow centres; petal size and leaf shape determine species.

**WHITE STONECROP**
*Sedum album*
Occasional on cliff rocks; dense prostrate plant; fleshy small egg-shaped leaves; abundant starry flowers slightly pink tinged. Jun-Aug.

## GRASS OF PARNASSUS
*Parnassia palustris*
Plentiful in flushes on boulder clay; from Jul-Oct cliffs are sprinkled with these beautiful white flowers, mauve-veined and yellow-centred; stems up to 25cm tall each have one clasping leaf and a single flower up to 30mm across; long-stalked leaves numerous at base. Not a grass, its name derives from Mount Parnassus where it was revered in Greek mythology 2,000 years ago.

## BROOKWEED
*Samolus valerandi*
Locally rare, confined to a few sea-sprayed gullies on exposed chalk cliffs at Flamborough. A well-named plant for it engulfs shallow rivulets with crowded leafy stems; fleshy spikes 10-20cm tall have clusters of small white 5 petalled flowers. Jun-Aug.

## WOOD SORREL *Oxalis acetosella*
Occasional in moist shady locations; also known as fairy bells, it covers the ground with short stalked, pale green shamrock leaves which fold back at dusk; single stemmed delicate flowers with 5 rounded white petals, streaked mauve; 10-20cm tall. Regarded as an indicator of an ancient woodland site. Apr-May.

## BLADDER CAMPION  *Silene vulgaris*
Occasional in rough ground; on tall erect hairless stems each short branch has a prominent inflated papery calyx topped by notched petals; greyish waxy leaves. May-Aug.

## WHITE CAMPION
*Silene latifolia*
Infrequent on disturbed ground; sticky, hairy plant up to 1m tall; flowers with narrow green calyx and rough leaves. May-Oct.

## WILD STRAWBERRY *Fragaria vesca*
With fruits like a miniature garden strawberry – and just as tasty – this plant sprawls on woodside, hedgebanks and cliff ledges; flowers up to 2cm across hide sepals beneath; large shiny leaflets in 3's have an obvious end point. Apr-Jul.

## BARREN STRAWBERRY *Potentilla sterilis*
As its name implies, no tasty red fruits on this plant which produces hard single-seeded fruits; slightly notched petals spaced to show sepals between; dull blue/green smaller leaves lack a prominent end point; low growing, frequent in scrub. Feb-May.

### COMMON CHICKWEED  *Stellaria media*

Is widespread in grassy ground; weak sprawling stem has a vertical line of hairs; green pointed sepals show between small white petals; flowers all year round.
**Lesser chickweed** *S. pallida* is a tiny annual with short green sepals, no petals; appears in pavement cracks. Feb-May.

### GREATER STITCHWORT  *S. holostea*

Is plentiful on grassy banks near hedge and copse; flowers 1.5-3cm across appear from Apr onwards; they are nearly twice the size of lesser stitchwort which flowers later.

### WOOD STITCHWORT

*S. nemorum*
Rare by shady stream at Staithes; long stalked, quite large leaves and flowers; hairy stems to 60cm. May-June.

### BOG STITCHWORT

*S. uliginosa*
Common in wet grassy places; square stems to 40cm; flowers look green striped with petals shorter than sepals. May-Jun.

### LESSER STITCHWORT

*S. graminea*
Starry flowers less than 2cm across with deeply cleft petals; a frequent weak-stemmed scrambler on acid grassland. May-Aug.

## mouse-ears  *Cerastium spp.* are short hairy plants with 5 styles

### COMMON MOUSE-EAR

*C. fontanum*
Is abundant on drier cliffs in grassy and rocky habitats; flowers in pairs; leaves <u>dull green</u> very hairy but not glandular; sprawling plant usually less than 20cm high. Apr-Sept.

### STICKY MOUSE-EAR

*C. glomeratum*
Is frequent on field edge and bare ground; flowers bunched together; leaves <u>yellowish-green</u> with gland-tipped hairs making it sticky to touch. Apr-Sept.

### FIELD MOUSE-EAR

*C. arvense*
Is infrequent on lime-rich grassland; upright to 20cm; has large flowers and hairy stem with downy linear leaves. Apr-Aug.

**Snow-in-summer** *C. tomentosum* is a rampant garden rockery plant naturalised on cliffs near habitation; narrow blue/grey leaves and large flowers.

### DROPWORT *Filipendula vulgaris*

An attractive herb confined to calcareous grassland eg on Tenants cliff, Cayton and on the Flamborough headland; creamy white flowers, pink in bud; stems to 40cm; leaves have up to 20 pairs of neatly toothed large and small leaflets. May-Aug.

### MEADOWSWEET *Filipendula ulmaria*

Widespread on marsh and cliff seepages; stems over 1m tall have frothy clusters of fragrant, cream, small flowers then spirally twisted fruits; pairs of toothed leaves, green above pale beneath, alternate large and small. A former strewing herb. Jun-Sep.

### WOOD ANEMONE *Anemone nemorosa*

Numerous in dappled shade these woodland spring flowers also survive harsh winds on exposed cliff grassland mainly north of Scalby. Up to 9 white petals are often pink beneath; short leafy carpeting plants.

### RAMSONS *Allium ursinum*

Leafy spring bulb with strong garlic smell; prefers lime-rich moist soil in shade; extensive woodland ground cover; long pointed leaves with parallel veins. Apr-Jun.

### SNOWDROP *Galanthus nivalis*

Extensive in shady damp woodland eg at Runswick Bay, Robin Hood's Bay and in cliff gullies; small bell-type flowers with 3 white sepals protecting 3 shorter inner petals, splashed green; flowers hang singly on short stems. Jan-Mar.

### LILY OF THE VALLEY *Convallaria majalis*

This plant of undisturbed ancient woodland now rare in the wild survives at Runswick Bay; frequent in gardens; fragrant small flowers hang on short spikes May-Jun; poisonous red berries later.

### LARGE BINDWEED *Calystegia sylvatica*

Introduced for gardens from southern Europe; now common in the wild; clambers over hedges and thickets; white trumpet flowers up to 6cm across have 2 large pointed bracts inflated to hide 5 calyx lobes. Jun-Sep.

### HEDGE BINDWEED *Calystegia sepium*

Is a native plant; smaller leaves and trumpets up to 4cm across with close fitting bracts which expose calyx lobes below; locally more frequent on the coast than inland but not common. Jul-Sep.

## composite flowers – daisy type

Flowerheads have many individual florets each containing stamens and a style; centre disc florets are tiny, petalless tubes; outer ray florets have a petal extension.

---

**SEA MAYWEED** *Tripleurospermum maritimum*
Common from high water to cliff top; bushy plant to 40cm; leaves <u>shiny</u> dark green finely divided into narrow, fleshy <u>blunt</u> segments; flowers have yellow centre disc and white outer 'petals'. Jul-Sep.

**Scentless mayweed** *T.inodorum* and **scented mayweed** *Matricaria recutita* are frequent on field edge; similar to **sea mayweed** but more upright to 60cm with <u>dull sharp pointed</u> leaf segments not fleshy. May onwards.

---

**OX-EYE DAISY** *Leucanthemum vulgare*
Scattered in cliff top meadows especially in conservation areas; large flowerheads 5cm across on stalks up to 70cm tall; May-Sep. Also known as moon or dog daisy.

**Shasta daisy** *Leucanthemum superbum*
Cliffs below some caravan sites have broad swathes of this garden flower; like ox-eye daisy but flowerheads up to 8cm across.

---

**FEVERFEW** *Tanacetum parthenium*
Its name indicates why this herb has long been grown in cottage gardens as a wide ranging medicinal remedy; strongly aromatic; escapes to walls and rough ground near houses; flowers white-petalled with yellow centres in sprays; bushy plant with yellowish-green ferny foliage. Jun-Aug.

**COMMON DAISY** *Bellis perennis*
A beautiful pink tinted flower often despised through over familiarity; from a ground rosette of spoon-shaped leaves, short stemmed flowers grow nearly all year round; rooting runners and prolific seeding make it plentiful in short grassland on cliff slopes and tops, lawns and verges; stays wintergreen.

**YARROW** *Achillea millefolium*
Very common in rough grassy places; tough downy stems to 45cm are topped with flattish spreads of small cream centred flowers; finely divided ferny dull green leaves. It had an ancient reputation for healing spear wounds. Jun-Sep.

**SNEEZEWORT** *Achillea ptarmica*
Rare in acid wet grassland and ditches; erect stems to 60cm have narrow dark green finely toothed leaves; daisy-type flowers with white outer petals, buff centre disc; acrid tasting leaves said to induce sneezing. Jul-Aug.

41

Plants in this group vary from short to over 2m tall and grow in a range of different habitats but all have small flowers arranged in flat or dome-shaped sprays at the ends of stems which radiate from a central stem like umbrella spokes; flowering time and fruits (shown below) are helpful for identification; most species are poisonous.

### COW PARSLEY
*Anthriscus sylvestris*
Also known as Queen Anne's lace from its frothy flower head; common on waysides; <u>stems ridged, hollow</u> 60-100cm. Apr-Jun.

### ROUGH CHERVIL
*Chaerophylum temulem*
Prefers light shade on non- acidic soil; scarce on the coast; <u>solid purple-spotted stem</u> hairy 30-90cm. May-Jul.

### UPRIGHT HEDGE PARSLEY
*Torilis japonica*
Frequent in rough grassy ground; <u>solid stems</u> up to 120 cm <u>tough and bristly;;</u> flowers pinkish; seeds with hooked spines. Jul-Sept.

### WILD CARROT
*Daucus carota*
Abundant on cliff slopes, scarce inland; white/pink domed flowerhead is concave in bud & fruit; centre flower often purple. Jun-Aug.

### SWEET CICELY
*Myrrhis odorata*
Occasional in damp shady places north of Scarborough; bright green leaves smell of aniseed; long narrow ridged fruits. May-Jul.

### HEMLOCK
*Conium maculatum*
Up to 2m tall, occasional on cliff tops; <u>purple blotched stems</u> hollow, hairless; foliage pale, finely divided; musty smelling, very poisonous. Jun-Jul.

### HEMLOCK WATER DROPWORT
*Oenanthe crocata*
Grows in salty grassland eg Ruswarp, Cayton; stems up to 2m are hollow, ridged, hairless; smells of parsley; very poisonous. Jun-Jul.

### TUBULAR WATER DROPWORT
*Oenanthe fistulosa*
Has greyish tall slender hollow stems, much <u>inflated</u> between leaf junctions. Scarce, known only in brackish cliff pools south of Filey. Jul-Sep.

**HOGWEED** *Heracleum sphondylium*
Robust plant up to 2m tall with rough, hairy, hollow stems, common in rank grassland; flowerhead ± flat, often pinkish, smells strongly of pigs; flowers produced almost throughout the year; leaves coarse, deeply lobed.

**ANGELICA** *Angelica sylvestris*
Prominent 2m tall plant frequent in wetland; large domed heads of pinkish/ white flowers on broad hollow stems; fleshy leaf stalks inflated around main stem; large leaflets on pinnate lower leaves. Jul-Aug.

**WILD CELERY** *Apium graveolens*
A plant of saline grassland eg creeks on Ruswarp Batts; grooved hollow flower stems to 60cm tall; familiar celery leaves and strong smell; sparse heads of greenish white small flowers Jun-Aug. Not common.

**GROUND ELDER** *Aegopodium podograria*
Rooting fragments of broken stems make this carpeting plant a serious garden weed; also frequent on grassy cliffs; pairs of large leaflets on long stalks, lower leaflet has extra 'thumb' lobe; dingy white flowers on hollow, hairless stems to 60cm. Jun-Jul.

**FOOLS WATERCRESS** *Apium nodiflorum* Water plant up to 1m tall; has 3-6 pairs of toothed bright green shiny leaflets; 0-2 bracts where flower stalks radiate from main stem; confused with and may grow with lesser water parsnip. Jun-Aug.

**LESSER WATER PARSNIP** *Berula erecta*
Poisonous waterside plant, not locally common; has a dark ring round lower leaf stalk; several bracts beneath flowers and 5-15 pairs of dull bluish leaflets distinguish it from fools watercress. Jul-Sep.

43

**SANICLE** *Sanicula europaea*
In woody shade on nutrient rich soil, eg Boggle Hole, Stoupe Beck; small globes of tiny dusky white flowers on stems to 50 cm; shiny, lobed leaves. May-Jul.

**PIGNUT** *Conopodium majus*
A low-medium slender wide-spread plant in short grassy ground; flowerheads on branched smooth stems up to 50cm; dark green leaves very finely divided; grows from small edible underground tubers once relished by free-ranging pigs. May-Jun.

**BURNET SAXIFRAGE**
*Pimpinella saxifraga*
Frequent on grassy calcareous cliff slopes; rough round stems 30-60cm with tiny flowers Jul-Aug; short linear upper leaves; lower leaves have pairs of toothed oval leaflets similar to leaves of burnet rose and salad burnet.

**WHITE DEADNETTLE**
*Lamium album*
Frequent in rank grassland on cliffs south of Scalby; large greenish white flowers have a divided lower lip and large hooded petal hiding black tipped stamens; these provide useful early pollen for bees as it flowers most of the year; 20-60cm tall square stems.

**HEMPNETTLE**
*Galeopsis tetrahit*
Rough hairy annual occasional in old quarries and waysides; whorls of small drab pinkish/cream flowers in bristly calyx tubes; square hairy stems to 1m tall are swollen beneath each pair of nettle-like but non-stinging leaves. Jul-Sep.

**WHITE CLOVER**
*Trifolium repens*
Abundant carpeting plant in grassland; mats of trifoliate leaves, each oval leaflet with a whitish crescent; small white pea-type florets packed in globular heads which turn brown and droop as they mature. Jun-Sept.

**EYEBRIGHT**
*Euphrasia sp*
Plentiful low-growing plant in turf eg Reighton undercliff; pairs of small fringed leaves clasp short stems with mauve/white flowers; used over centuries and still valued as an eye-lotion ingredient. Jun-Oct.

**KNOTGRASS**
*Polygonum aviculare*
Low-growing wiry plant common on bare ground including sea shore above high water; easily overlooked with short grassy leaves and insignificant green/white flowers held close to long creeping or erect stems. Jun-Oct.

## DOGS MERCURY *Mercurialis perennis*

Frequent north of Filey Bay; forms large colonies mainly in light woodland shade and on cliff ledges;

unbranched stem 15-40cm tall has pairs of faintly toothed thin leaves and short flowering spikes from Feb to early summer; male (above) or female (left) small greenish flowers on separate plants. Like dog daisy or dog rose, there is no canine connection – 'dog' implies common or everyday.

## BLACK BRYONY *Tamus communis*

'Black' refers to hidden roots; small pale yellowish/green male and female flowers often on same plant; more noticeable are shiny heart-shaped

leaves and scarlet berries; long stems twine up hedgerows but avoid wet ground; a southern species near its northern limit.

## NETTLE *Urtica dioica*

Widespread in bare and grassy waste; spreads into large stands; stems over 1m tall and leaves have hairs with a stinging juice; tiny green flowers on short dangling

stems Jun-Aug. Fibrous nettle stems were once woven into fabric; leaves still used for making soup or tea.

**SMALL NETTLE** *Urtica urens* Summer annual of disturbed ground occasional on field edge; half the size of common nettle; leaves longer stalked and more deeply toothed.

## PARSLEY PIERT *Aphanes arvensis*

A ground-hugging small annual with tiny almost hidden flowers; many neatly toothed roundish leaves only 2-10mm across form large mats in bare or short grassy ground. Apr-Oct. Its name is corrupted from the French *perce-pierre* meaning stone breaker – no connection with edible parsley.

## PEARLWORTS *Sagina spp.*

Often mistaken for a moss, these common low matted plants creep around paving and bare ground; named from the tiny pale seed capsule which surmounts 4 or 5 green sepals; short linear leaves; petals often missing; flowers May-Sep.

**annual pearlwort**
*S. apetala*
Usually has 4 sepals, no petals and all shoots producing flowers.

**procumbent pearlwort**
*S. procumbens*
Is a perennial with a few non-flowering shoots, 4 or 5 sepals; petals absent or tiny.

45

**FAT-HEN or GOOSEFOOT** *Chenopodium album*
A widespread annual weed on waste ground; short-medium upright, often reddish, stems; greyish leaves, linear at top, broad below; tiny inconspicuous flowers; small rough <u>rounded</u> fruits differ from angular fruits of

oraches.'Fat-hen' is a reminder of lean times when its mealy fruits were gathered for poultry feed; 'goosefoot' indicates the lower leaf shape of members of this family. Jul-Oct.

**PRICKLY SALTWORT** *Salsola kali*
Rare on this coast, last recorded at Scarborough in 1912 until a single plant was found in Cayton Bay in 2004. A strand line plant of sandy shores; tiny 5 petalled flowers grow at the base of fleshy bluish leaves, each strongly spine-tipped. Jul-Oct.

# oraches *Atriplex spp.*

Sprawling weedy plants able to flourish both in disturbed ground and on tidal shores; inconspicuous flowers on leafy spikes produce green fleshy fruits like small triangular envelopes; often grows in extensive colonies. Jul-Oct.

### COMMON ORACHE
*A. patula*
Has triangular lower leaves tapering into the stalk, lobes forward pointing; fruits smooth.

### SPEAR-LEAVED ORACHE
*A. prostrata*
Has triangular lower leaves which form a right-angle join with the stem, lobes point downwards; fruits wrinkled.

### GRASS-LEAVED ORACHE
*A. littoralis*
Has narrow linear leaves and is a more upright greyish plant. Often prolific in the splash zone of salted roads.

### FROSTED ORACHE
*A. laciniata*
An infrequent strandline plant with reddish stems and diamond-shaped leaves mealy coated to appear silver white. Close to the cliffs on Cayton and Reighton shores.

# orchids

### TWAYBLADE *Listera ovata*
This sturdy orchid up to 60cm is recognisable by

its 2 large parallel-veined oval leaves which encircle the lower stem; green flowers have long divided lower lip; small groups grow on grassy cliff slopes, hedge banks, woodside. Jun-Jul.

### FROG ORCHID *Coeloglossum viride*
With greenish flowers and foliage and less

than 20cm tall this is a difficult orchid to find in grassy places; more obvious on stony ground; prefers lime rich soils; grows on rock ledges at Beast cliff and an old railtrack embankment at Ravenscar. Jun-Aug.

### REEDMACE *Typha latifolia*
Large stands of this impressive plant grow in some undercliff swamps and clifftop pools; up to 2.5m tall, stout, round stems are topped by a short spike of pale male flowers contiguous with a long dense tube of velvet brown female flowers; these ripen into fluffy 'parachute'

seeds once used as mattress stuffing; broad greyish twisted tough leaves. Jun-Jul.

### COMMON REED *Phragmites australis*
Frequent and often in extensive colonies beside streams cutting through cliffs towards the shore eg Primrose Valley; sturdy stems reach over 3m, topped by waving plumes of purplish brown silky florets. Aug-Oct.

### BRANCHED BUR-REED *Sparganium erectum*
Occasional in shallow water in cliff streams and pools eg Cayton shore; amidst bright green waving leaves are branched stems, 60-100cm tall, with globes of tiny flowers which mature into green prickly balls of fruits. Jun-Aug.

### REED CANARY GRASS *Phalaris arundinacea*
Grows in dense stands by a few streams and cliff pools; stems up to 2m tall carry loose bunches of pale geenish, quickly maturing spikelets; broad rough leaves. More familiar in a variegated form as a garden plant. Jun-Aug.

# club rushes

Conspicuous wetland plants up to 3m tall make impressive stands in brackish or slow moving water eg Cayton shore pool and Ruswarp Batts.

## COMMON CLUB RUSH
*Schoenoplectus lacustris*
Has smooth rounded stems; spreading clusters of spikelets; short leaf-like bract above spikelets.

## SEA CLUB RUSH
*Bolboschoenus maritimus*
Has triangular, rough stems; tight cluster of spikelets; long tapering bract above spikelets.

# horsetails

*Equisetum spp* Perennial wetland colonial plants on undercliffs and in shallow pools; jointed hollow stems may have whorls of linear branches; slender cones at the tops of fertile, often pinkish, stems produce ripe spores early summer.

### GREAT HORSETAIL *E. telmateia*
Large stands are common on slumped boulder clay; whitish-green thick barren stems up to 2m tall; shorter fat fertile stems up to 40cm. This large dominant horsetail often indicates water exuding from a springline on the cliffs.

### WATER HORSETAIL *E.fluviatile*
Forms dense patches in standing or slow moving water; bright green stems with large central hollow feel fragile; 60-130cm.

### MARSH HORSETAIL
*E. palustre* grows in wetland; dark green stems feel stiff with small central hollow. 10-60cm.

### FIELD HORSETAIL *E. arvense*
A common and often troublesome creeping perennial of damp grassland; fertile cone-bearing stems 10-25cm in March are followed by dull green sterile stems up to 80cm; feels coarse.

### WOOD HORSETAIL *E. sylvaticum*
An elegant horsetail in moist acidic woodlands north of Filey; both fertile and barren stems are yellowish green, up to 80cm, and have drooping slender branches to give a feathery appearance.

**grasses** are prolific opportunist plants which account for a large proportion of coastal vegetation; adapted to a range of habitats, grass species vary in size and form to create an almost contiunuous backdrop for more colourful flowering plants. Upwards of 30 species include **sweet vernal grass**, **sterile**, **hairy** and **false bromes**, **crested dogstail**, **meadow** and **marsh foxtail**, **red** and **sheep's fescue**, **wood melick**, **soft grasses**, **ryegrass**, **meadowgrasses**, **sweetgrass**, **hairgrasses**, **yellow oatgrass**, **Yorkshire fog**, **creeping softgrass**, **bentgrasses**, **timothy**, and **purple moorgrass**. A changing mosaic of

grassland ranges from tall rank vegetation dominated by **false oatgrass** and **tall fescue** to widespread pastureland where **red fescue** and **creeping bent** create dense tangled ground cover. Extensive on some sea-sprayed cliffs is a bluish-grey hue where **red fescue** has adapted to avoid dessication by salt-laden seaspray; this strategy is seen also by tall glaucous shoreline grasses – **marram**, **lymegrass** and **sand couch**. More specialised grasses (described below) appear in small numbers in some unusual habitats which the coastline provides.

## shore grasses – tall

**MARRAM**
*Ammophila arenaria*
Forms large tussocks on upper sandy shores; dense cylinder of pale hairy spikelets on long stems; tightly inrolled leaves, shiny outside, have long sharp points. Jul-Aug.

**LYMEGRASS**
*Leymus arenarius*
Robust very glaucous plant; spikelets densely crowded and flattened all round the stems which exceed 1m tall; makes large stands with wide bluish leaves; prominent on Sands-end shore. Jun-Aug.

**SAND COUCH** *Elytrigia juncea* has spikelets in 2 rows on opposite sides of the stem; they lie alternately from side to side and evenly spaced from top to bottom; high salt tolerance allows growth near to the sea when its leaves are inrolled and glaucous.
**COMMON COUCH** *Elytrigia repens* is very common in rough and cultivated ground; also known as wickens or twitch, it closely resembles and often grows alongside **sand couch** but has less hairy, usually flat green leaves.

## cliff grasses – tall

**FALSE OATGRASS**
*Arrhenatherum elatius*
An attractive waving grass up to 1.5m tall common on cliffs; nodding flowerheads have shining green/ purplish spikelets each with a projecting awn. Jun-Sep. Finely pointed rough leaves.

**COCKSFOOT**
*Dactylis glomerata*
A coarse widespread grass with globular clusters of spikelets on wavy stalks; forms tufts of 1m tall flower stems with rough-edged leaves, folded flat in bud. May onwards.

**TALL FESCUE**
*Festuca arundinacea*
A rough tufted grass up to 2m tall, wide-spread on cliff tops and basins; wide, finely pointed leaves have a fringe (auricle) of short hairs where they join the stem; flowers Jun-Aug.

## cliff grasses – medium to short

**RED FESCUE**
*Festuca rubra*
Abundant on cliff tops
and slopes; flat leaves
on flowering shoots
amidst tufts of inrolled
wiry leaves are often
blue/grey ; 10-40cm tall.
May-Jun.

**CREEPING BENT** *Agrostis stolonifera*
Has masses of tiny
spikelets which give the
flowering stems a misty
shimmering effect;
matted carpets of rooting
leafy stolons extensive in
damp grass and waste
ground. Closely related
**common bent** is
frequent on dry acidic
ground. 10-60cm.
Jun-Aug.

**FERN GRASS**
*Catapodium rigidum*
Grows on sandy ground
and walls; rigid flat
flowerheads up to 20cm
erect or prostrate.
May-Jun.

**RATSTAIL FESCUE**
*Vulpia myuros*
Thrives in
warm dry
railtrack
ballast;
long-
awned
spikelets
on one side of 30cm
stems. Jun-Jul.

**QUAKING GRASS**
*Briza media*
Frequent on cliff clay
slumps;
small oval
spikelets
dangle on
slender
stems.
Jun-Jul.

**WALL
BARLEY**
*Hordeum
murinum*
Plentiful on
waste ground
especially old
rail ballast and
around
Scarborough
castle ramparts; pale
green flowerheads on
stems up to 50cm have
long-awned spikelets.
May-Aug.

**HAIRGRASS**
*Aira spp.* Both
**silver** and
**early hairgrass**
common on
sandy ground
eg railtrack; short thin
stems. Apr-Jun.

Infrequent grasses of specialised habitats are:
**saltmarsh grasses** *(Puccinellia spp.)* in salty
mud on shores and on the sides of salted roads
**heathgrass** *(Danthonia decumbens)* on damp
heath and sandy cliffs eg Reighton undercliff
**hardgrass** *(Paraphilos strigosa)* on sandy hillocks
along Sandsend shore
**whorlgrass** *(Catabrosa aquatica)* known only on
Saltwick undercliff.

# rushes
*Juncus spp.* Hairless perennials widespread on damp ground; long thin tubular leaves hollow or
pith-filled; clusters of small brown flowers in 6 segments (tepals); sizes vary from small prostrate to 100cm tall.

**SOFT RUSH** *J.effusus*
Very common in marsh and wet
grassland; stems up to 150cm are
smooth, shiny and pith filled;
'seaves' were once cut and peeled
to use the pith as rush-lamp wicks.

**COMPACT RUSH**
*J. conglomeratus* is like soft
rush but has a rough ridged
stem and tightly packed
flowerhead.

**HARD RUSH**
*J. inflexus* Has hard ridged grey-
green stems to 120 cm; prefers
limey soils.

**MUD RUSH** *J. gerardii*
Spreads extensively in
brackish mud eg Carr
Nase cliff pool and
Ruswarp Batts; up to
50cm stems; flattish
dark green leaves
only 1mm wide;
flowers small, shiny
brown.

Frequent rushes in
acid wetland are:
**sharp-flowered
rush** (erect
to100cm) and
**jointed rush** (to
60cm, stems
curve); both have
open spreadng
flowerheads and
leaves with
horizontal notches
which can be felt
by running a leaf
between finger
and thumb. Rarely
more than 10cm
high in muddy
tracks and pools
are **toad rush** and
**bulbous rush.**

# arrowgrasses

*Triglochin spp.*
Not a grass despite the name and grass-like leaves; these upright plants resemble plantains with unbranched erect stems and inconspicuous flowers but they have no ground rosette of leaves, lack obvious stamens and always grow in wet ground. 15-40cm.

### SEA ARROWGRASS
*T. maritima*
Has leaves flat above and rounded beneath; tiny flowers packed up the stem; narrow fruits fall off when ripe; grows where saltwater penetrates. Jul-Sep.

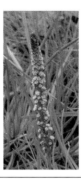

### MARSH ARROWGRASS
*T. palustris*
Has fleshy linear leaves grooved above, rounded below; tiny globular flowers spaced up the stem; thin oval fruits open at base to form arrow shape; grows in wet grassland and cliff marshes. Jun-Aug.

## sedges
*Carex spp.* have triangular solid stems, grass-like leaves and packed heads of tiny petalless flowers. Growth form, habitat and structure of leaves, stem and fruits are needed for identification. Of 36 species known to grow in north-east Yorkshire at least 12 occur along the coast. Commonest of these are **pendulous, glaucous** and **false fox sedges.** Others in coastal vegetation include hairy, sand, distant, common, smooth-stalked, oval, remote, carnation, wood and yellow sedges.

### PENDULOUS SEDGE *C. pendula*
An impressive plant of damp woods and stream banks. Up to 2m tall it carries long waving tawny spikes May-Jul; wide rough-edged glossy green leaves; grows in most coastal wood-land often in deep shade.

### GLAUCOUS SEDGE
*C. flacca*
Makes blue/grey leafy carpets on wet clay cliffs; leaves glaucous below, green above; nodding lower spike. 10-40cm. May-Aug.

### FALSE FOX SEDGE
*C. otrubae*
Large tufts up to 1m tall are frequent on damp cliffs; bright green leaves surround tall spikes of angular fruits. Jul-Sep.

## woodrushes
*Luzula spp.* have flat grass-like leaves fringed with long white hairs; clustered flowerheads.

### FIELD WOODRUSH or GOOD FRIDAY GRASS
*L. campestris*
Stems up to 15cm with 1 sessile and 3-6 short stalked flower clusters; dangling stamens; common in grassy places. Apr-May.

### HEATH WOODRUSH
*L. multiflora*
Stems 20-40cm; 8-16 flower clusters both stalked and non-stalked; stamens ± sessile; common on acid heath. May-Jun.

### GREAT WOODRUSH *L. sylvatica*
Large tufted plant widespread on older undercliffs from Cloughton northwards avoiding lime-rich soils. Bright green leaves form dense stands; clusters of ginger brown flowers May-Jun.

**SPURGE LAUREL** *Daphne laureola*
This native fragrant evergreen shrub is reaching its northern UK limit, growing in old deciduous woodland at Runswick and Sandsend. It forms a lax open shrub up to 1m high; by February its greenish/yellow small trumpet flowers emerge in clusters amongst long shiny leaves followed by black globular fruits.

**WALLFLOWER** *Erysimum cheiri*
Frequent on old walls of Whitby Abbey and Scarborough Castle. Mustard yellow flowers and narrow grey/green leaves grow from tough woody stems. Mar-Jun.

**TORMENTIL** *Potentilla erecta*
Frequent thoughout on meadow and heathland; small 'square' flowers face skywards above a creeping mat of foliage; 3 or 5 lobed deeply toothed leaflets. Jun-Sep. (*See also creeping cinquefoil*)

**LADY'S BEDSTRAW**
*Galium verum*
Widespread in large patches on cliff tops and rocky outcrops; tiny bright yellow flowers in loose clusters on many short branches Jul-Aug; up to 12 hairy linear leaflets in whorls on square stems.

**CROSSWORT**
*Cruciata laevipes*
Frequent on path and woodland edge; square stems erect to 60cm have several whorls of 4 hairy oval pointed leaflets; tiny yellow, scented flowers clustered above each whorl Apr-Jun.

**GOLDEN SAXIFRAGE** *Chrysosplenium spp.* Two closely allied and sometimes intermixed ground cover plants of wet shady ground and flushes; stems 5-15cm; small yellow/green flowers Apr-May.

**Opposite leaved golden saxifrage** has small wedge-shaped leaves growing in pairs. Common and extensive in marshland.

**Alternate leaved golden saxifrage** is less frequent; has larger circular sparsely hairy leaves growing singly. Flowers somewhat brighter.

**EASTERN ROCKET** *Sisymbrium orientale*
Annual from southern Europe rare in this area, occurs around Whitby and Scarborough harbours; very long narrow pods on med-tall branched hairy plant; few pale yellow flowers. Jun-Aug.

**HEDGE MUSTARD** *Sisymbrium officinale*
Common throughout on rough or bare ground; large hairy plant with wide angled branches; narrow seed pods held close to stems; small flowers appear all summer; rough deeply lobed basal leaves; stiff ungainly plant 30-90cm.

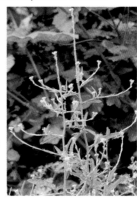

**WILD CABBAGE** *Brassica oleracea*
Uncommon native coastal plant near Whitby and Staithes on rocky cliffs; originator of culinary 'greens'; large crinkle edged slaty blue fleshy leaves; pale yellow flowers May-Aug.

**WINTERCRESS** *Barbarea spp.*
Occasional plants on damp ground by paths and roadside verges; shiny dark green lobed leaves; erect stems to 90cm clustered with small flowers May-Aug.

**CHARLOCK** *Sinapis arvensis*
Frequent on cliff tops where land is farmed to the cliff edge; spreads downslope with cliff falls; a persistent rough hairy plant 30-60cm tall with bristly leaves; flowers in many loose bunches May-Aug; cylindrical pods tapered into pointed beaks.

**WALL ROCKET** *Diplotaxis muralis*
Infrequent on derelict buildings and waste ground; basal rosette of small lobed leaves; lemon yellow flowers on long stalks; slender pods narrowed at each end. Jun Sep.

**SILVERWEED** *Potentilla anserina*
Common spreading low plant on sandy shores and turf; silvery <u>pinnate</u> leaves with neatly toothed leaflets form dense mats; flowers with <u>rounded</u> petals single on long stalks. May-Aug.

**CREEPING CINQUEFOIL** *Potentilla reptans*
Common on pathsides and bare ground; low creeping plant; cinquefoil differs from silverweed by <u>notched</u> petals and all green leaves <u>palmately</u> divided. May-Oct.

# buttercups *Ranunculus spp.* One or more of these adaptable species can be found in most of the varied habitats along the coast; closely allied are the white-flowered water crowfoots which grow in damp or marshy areas. *(See also celandine, a member of the ranunculus family with 7-12 petals)*

**CREEPING BUTTERCUP**
*R. repens* Spreading plant abundant in grassy ground; flower stalk <u>grooved</u>; hairy leaves have stalked centre leaflet. May-Aug.

**MEADOW BUTTERCUP**
*R. acris* Frequent in meadows; flower stalk <u>not grooved</u>, to 60cm tall; leaves palmately divided. May-Aug.

**LESSER SPEARWORT**
*R. flammula* Frequent in wetland; hollow stems creep over wide area; long narrow oval leaves. May-Sept.

**BULBOUS BUTTERCUP**
*R. bulbosus*
Common on dry grassland; deep yellow flowers, sepals reflexed; <u>grooved stalks.</u> Mar-Jun.

**CELERY LEAVED BUTTERCUP**
*R. sceleratus*
Patchy in muddy ponds at Whitby, Ruswarp, Cayton; fleshy leaves; small shiny flowers. May-Sept.

**GOLDILOCKS**
*R. auricomus*
Woodland buttercup rarely grows 5 full petals; leaves linear on stem, lobed at base. Apr-Jun.

**PRIMROSE** *Primula vulgaris*
Abundant on moist cliffs and in woods; ground rosettes of crinkled spoon-shaped leaves hairless above; single flowers on long hairy stems; petals slightly notched.
Mar-Jun.

**COWSLIP** *Primula veris*
Prefers light soils, infrequent on coastal boulder clay; bunches of short-stalked flowers hang from single stems; small petals fringe a tube enclosed by a pale green calyx; leaves hairy above. Apr-May.

**BARBERRY** *Berberis vulgaris*
Owing to its association with a cereal fungus, most barberry shrubs have been removed from farmed areas; a few survive in woods around Runswick, Ravenscar and Sandsend. Between short spines and toothed oval leaves hang sprays of small cup-shaped flowers May-Jun; red oval berries follow.

**GOOSEBERRY** *Ribes uva-crispa*
A spiny garden shrub occasional in scrub or hedgerow; 5 lemon/pink petals are reflexed on small flowers in spring followed by familiar green gooseberries.

**WALL LETTUCE** *Mycelis muralis*
Occurs in the few suitable habitats – moist woody shade and on lime-rich rocks and walls; a spindly hairless plant to 1m tall; few small daisy type flowers each with 5 strap florets or 'petals'. Jun-Sep.

**WOOD AVENS** *Geum urbanum*
Frequent on woodland edge and cliff top scrub; hairy wide-branched plant to 60cm tall; single stemmed starry flowers under 1cm across show green sepals between spaced deep yellow petals; leaves divided and tooth-edged; distinctive burr fruits. May-Aug.

**MULLEIN**
*Verbascum thapsus*
Old alum works at Ravenscar provide suitable dry stony habitat for this handsome opportunist plant; amidst large felted leaves grow thick stems up to 2m tall densely packed towards the top with 5-petalled flowers. June-Aug.

**AGRIMONY**
*Agrimonia spp.*
Scattered in grassy scrub; small 5 petalled flowers closely surround upper stems; large and small toothed leaflets alternate on long stalks; small oval fruits ringed with hooked hairs pointing forwards on **common agrimony** but spreading outwards and backwards on lemon scented **fragrant agrimony;** upright and branched to 80cm. Jun-Aug.

**ROCKROSE** *Helianthemum nummularium*
Rare on this coast, known only from Hunmanby Gap and Tan Beck valley Ravenscar; flowers to 2.5cm across have thin papery petals; paired narrow oval leaves are woolly white beneath; tangles of low sprawling leafy stems. May-Sept.

**MARSH MARIGOLD** *Caltha palustris*
Marnardale in Robin Hood's Bay has the marshy streamside where 'kingcups' thrives; infrequent on the coast; large bright 5-petalled flowers bloom from March to mid-summer; cordate glossy green leaves on fleshy single stalks.

# pansies *Viola spp* Woodland violets have purple or white petals, heart-shaped leaves. Open ground pansies are pale yellow with or without purple tints; leaves spoon-shaped, wavy-edged stipules.

**FIELD PANSY** *V. arvensis*
A short annual common on arable fields; flowers 8-20mm pale yellow or mauve tinted; green pointed sepals show between petals. Apr-Oct.

**WILD PANSY** *V. tricolor*
A plant of arable land and short turf, locally rare; flowers 20-30mm hide sepals beneath; petals various shades of yellow and mauve. Apr-Sep.

# St John's worts

*Hypericum spp.* Occasional on path, railtrack or wood edge; branched often reddish stems have paired smooth-edged leaves; starry flowers usually with numerous stamens and petals with black dots. Named after Knights of St John who believed in the healing powers of these plants when injured on Crusades. Still used medicinally.

### PERFORATE ST JOHN'S WORT *H. perforatum*

Hairless stem has <u>2 raised ridges</u>; flowers bright yellow about 2cm; needs well-drained ground; 30-90cm. Jun-Sep.

### HAIRY ST JOHN'S WORT *H. hirsutum*

Has <u>hairy</u> leaves and <u>round</u> stems to 60cm; flowers pale yellow to 2cm across; damp non-acid soils. Jul-Aug.

### SQUARE-STALKED ST JOHN'S WORT *H. tetrapterum*

Hairless stem with <u>4 raised ridges</u>; flowers pale yellow 1cm across; grows in damp places; 80cm. Jun-Sep.

### TUTSAN

*H. androsaemum*

Rare shrub in ancient woodland eg Boggle Hole and Ravenscar; often planted in gardens; reddish 2-ridged stems have groups of flowers 15 – 25mm; red berries turn black. Jun-Aug

### TRAILING ST JOHN'S WORT *H. humifusum*

Uncommon low trailing plant on acid heathland and old railtrack; flowers up to 1cm cover unequal sepals; rather narrow small leaves; wiry stems 2 ridged. Jun-Sep.

### SLENDER STJOHN'S WORT *H. pulchrum*

A plant with deep yellow petals, red buds; round hairless reddish erect stems to 40cm; small blunt triangular paired leaves; on acid heath or peaty habitats. Jul-Aug.

### BITING STONECROP *Sedum acre*

Low growing plant on dry gravel and stony outcrops; acrid tasting oval succulent leaves form dense mats; small starry flowers. Jun-Jul.

### YELLOW PIMPERNEL *Lysimachia nemorum*

Short hairless perennial spreads over woodland floors; delicate stalks with starry flowers rise between paired oval leaves. May-Sept.

## YELLOWWORT
*Blackstonia perfoliata*
In small populations on lime-rich slumped cliffs and spring outlets, rare inland locally. Pairs of greyish waxy leaves encircle 15-40cm stems; neat 6-8 petalled flowers. Jun-Sept.

## LESSER CELANDINE *Ranunculus ficaria*
Common in wood edge, short grassland and on cliff slopes. Single flowers deep yellow 7-12 petalled on hairless stems; cordate leaves dark green, often blotched. Up to 20cm tall. Feb-Jun.

## ALEXANDERS
*Smyrnium olusatrum*
The bright yellow green foliage and flowers of this Roman introduction are widespread from early April

and a prominent feature of coastal vegetation until mid-summer; a native of Macedonia it is rarely seen more than a mile inland in this region. Tall robust plant with branched furrowed stems and large celery-like leaves; said to have been used both medicinally and as a cooking herb.

## WILD PARSLEY *Petroselinum crispum*
Grows on Staithes Cowbar; solid stems and strong parsley smell distinguish it from wild celery; leaves not as crisped as garden parsley; flat head of yellowish flowers with forked bracts beneath. Jun-Aug.

## PEPPER SAXIFRAGE *Silaum silaus*
A lowland plant of damp natural grassland, locally rare; grows at Upgang and on Gristhorpe cliffs; tall branched rigid stems up to 90cm; leaves finely divided; flowers pale yellow soon fade. Jun-Aug.

## composite flowers

Flowerheads have many individual small florets clustered onto a flattish circular receptacle; each floret has stamens and a style in a small tube; **ray florets** have a petal-like extension; **disc florets** have no 'petal' extension.

**daisy** type flowers have ray florets with 'petals' round the edge of a dense centre of disc florets:

coltsfoot
fleabane
golden rod
coastal gum plant
leopardsbane
carline thistle
ragworts
groundsels (may lack ray 'petals' and appear as button type)

**dandelion** type flowers consist of ray florets only – no central disc florets:

stem unbranched
 goatsbeard
 dandelion
 catsear (also branched)
 mouse-ear hawkweed
 hairy hawkbit
 lesser hawkbit
stem branched
 hawkweeds
 sowthistles
 hawksbeards
 nipplewort
 oxtongue
 autumn hawkbit
 catsear

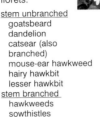

**button** type flowers consist of disc florets only and no ray florets with 'petals':

tansy
pineappleweed
groundsels (may have very short 'petals')

### composite flowers – button type

**TANSY**
*Tanacetum vulgare*
Occasional but nowhere plentiful;1m tall leafy clumps are topped with flat plates of small 'button' flowers Jul-Sept; neatly toothed ferny leaves; strongly aromatic plant used in cooking and medicine.

**PINEAPPLE WEED** *Matricaria discoidea*
A fruity smell surrounds these short ferny-leaved plants; abundant on trampled ground; branched stems have numerous small egg-shaped dense flowerheads most of the year.

### composite flowers – daisy type

**COMMON GROUNDSEL**
*Senecio vulgaris*
Widespread; flowers ± all year; florets on 40cm stems have tube of green bracts, black tipped at base; tiny or 0 ray florets.

**STICKY GROUNDSEL**
*Senecio viscosus*
Favours bare dry ground and has recurved ray florets; very sticky foetid hairy leaves and stem; up to 60cm. Jul-Sept.

**HEATH GROUNDSEL**
*Senecio sylvaticus*
Occasional on acid sandy soils; resembles sticky groundsel but yellowish leaves cottony beneath, not sticky .

**COMMON RAGWORT** *Senecio jacobaea*
Common bushy plant in rough grassland; loose sprays of deep yellow flowers on leafy branches May-Oct; leaves divided into many unequal lobes.

**HOARY RAGWORT** *S. erucifolius*
Common on cliffs and field edge; differs from common ragwort by paler yellow flowers and angular equal leaf lobes. Jul-Sept.

**MARSH RAGWORT** *S.aquaticus*
Uncommon marsh plant; large flowerheads to 3cm across; leaves only slightly divided have large end lobe. Jul-Aug.

**OXFORD RAGWORT** *S.squalidus*
Frequent on bare ground usually near habitation; differs from common ragwort by outer bracts beneath flowers all <u>black-tipped</u>; flowers slightly larger, brighter yellow, appear from Apr onwards.

**LEOPARDSBANE** *Doronicum pardalianches*
Clumps of this 1m tall garden plant occasional on cliffs near dwellings; large flowers on single stems May-Jul; long-stalked cordate leaves.

**CARLINE THISTLE** *Carlina vulgaris*
Common in drier non-acid ground; buff bracts resembling ray florets surround a centre disc of straw yellow florets; Jul-Oct; prickly leaves often cottony below; stems 10-60cm.

## composite flowers – daisy type

**COLTSFOOT** *Tussilago farfara*
Common on most cliffs where pieces of rooting stems are eroded down slope and soon start
new colonies; by Jan, flowers unfurl on short stems clad with fleshy scales; as flowerheads mature into white fluffy seedheads leaves emerge, green above, white felted below, shaped vaguely like a colt's foot.

**FLEABANE** *Pulicaria dysenterica*
Spreads widely over damp cliff slopes; golden yellow flowers at the tops of branched stems
Jul-Sept; hairy blunt-pointed leaves are greyish below and wavy-edged; 'parachute' type seeds enable this plant to colonise new slumps of seeping boulder clay quickly; 30-60cm.

**GOLDEN ROD** *Solidago virgaurea*
Scattered in grassy places on cliff tops and slopes; leafy branched stems to 50cm tall have
sprigs of short-stalked flowers; a few ray florets have wide spaced rather uneven 'petals' arround small centre discs. Jul-Sept.

**COASTAL GUM PLANT** *Grindelia stricta*
In UK the only known site for this North American plant is on rock outcrops where
Whitby west cliff abuts the harbour; in July it grows a mass of bright yellow flowers; apparently increasing since first recorded in 1977.

## composite flowers – dandelion type

**NIPPLEWORT** *Lapsana communis*
Frequent med-tall annual of grassy and bare places; much branched tough stems each have a small flower which opens only in sunlight before midday; thin hairy lower leaves are toothed and lobed. Jun-Sep. (*See also wall lettuce*)

**BRISTLY OXTONGUE** *Picris echioides*
This robust plant to 70cm tall is near its northern limit; infrequent on waste or bare ground eg near Boulby mine and re-aligned cliffs elsewhere; bristly hairs grow from pale leaf pimples and on stems. Jun-Oct.

# sowthistles

*Sonchus spp.* are robust plants with hollow branched stems and prickly stem leaves; often over 1m tall; three species are locally common in rough grass or waste land.

### PRICKLY SOWTHISTLE
*S. asper*

<u>Glossy</u> leaves, edges sharp spine-toothed; <u>rounded</u> leaf bases part cover the stem.
Jun-Oct.

### SMOOTH SOWTHISTLE
*S. oleraceus*

<u>Dull</u> green leaves with soft spined edge; <u>pointed</u> leaf bases clasp stems.
Jun-Oct.

### PERENNIAL or CORN SOWTHISTLE
*S. arvensis*

Up to 2m tall; large raggy flowers; stem and dark green sepals covered with <u>sticky orange glandular hairs</u>. Abundant on Filey Carr Nase.

### GOATSBEARD
*Tragopogon pratensis*
Long grass-like leaves and sepals almost hide large flowers of 'Jack-go-to-bed-at-noon' when they close around midday; stems up to 1m tall; small groups scattered in rank grassland all along the coast. Jun-Jul.

### HAWKWEED
*Hieracium sp.*
Med-tall leafy stemmed erect plants with branched stems; in colonies occasional on rocky banks or railtrack edge; leaves are mostly stalkless not lobed but slighlty tooth-edged; a variable species.
Jul-Oct.

### MOUSE-EAR HAWKWEED
*Pilosella officinarum*
Long leafy runners carpet extensively across dry stony ground and heath; common throughout; whiitish hairs on stems and leaves which are <u>felted beneath</u>; short erect stems have single pale yellow flowers streaked red below. May-Aug.

**DANDELION** *Taraxacum officinale*
Common in grassland; single flowers on short unbranched stems filled with milky latex; thin toothed leaves grow from ground rosette.
Mar-Oct.

## BRANCHED STEMS

**HAWKSBEARD**
*Crepis capillaris*
Common on cliff tops and slopes; flowers only ±1cm across are numerous on branched stems; a few bracts beneath flowers curve outwards; leaves stalkless, shiny, wavy-edged have forward projecting points. Jun-Oct.

**MARSH HAWKSBEARD**
*Crepis paludosa*
An upland species mainly north of Whitby; confined to a few wooded streamsides; thin hairless leaves clasp stems with long pointed lobes; large raggy flowers. Jul-Sep.

**CATSEAR**  *Hypochaeris radicata*
Common in grassland; rough hairy rosette leaves; flowerhead 2.5-4cm greyish beneath, sits squarely on branched or unbranched stem (hawkbit flowerheads taper); stem has small bracts or 'catsears'; 20-40cm. Jun-Sep.

**AUTUMN HAWKBIT** *Leontodon autumnalis*
Widespread on cliffs and grassy slopes; hairless, branched stems to 40cm often curved; flowerheads about 2cm red beneath. Jun-Oct.

## UNBRANCHED STEMS

**HAIRY HAWKBIT** *Leontodon hispidus*
Frequent in most grassland; hairy leaves form ground rosette; flowerhead 2.5-4cm across bronze beneath. stems to 60cm. Jun-Sep.

**LESSER HAWKBIT** *Leontondon saxatilis*
On short dry heath and stony ground eg Reighton undercliff; flowerheads up to 3cm across greyish mauve beneath; stems to 40cm. Jun-Sep.

**pea-type flowers** have one petal which forms an upright 'standard' at the top, 2 'wing' petals at the side and 2 lower petals making a 'keel'; in some species many small flowers are packed to form a globular head eg clovers and medicks.

**GORSE** *Ulex europaeus*
A strong almond scent fills the air around bushes of gorse during its spring flowering; large spiny shrubs make dense thickets on dry soils especially on old rail ballast and alum waste; ripe pods can be heard cracking open to release seeds; although Mar-June is the usual flowering time, its ability to bloom all year round has given rise to the old adage 'kissing is out of season when gorse is not in flower'. It has also caused confusion with a few western gorse *Ulex gallii* found near Staintondale which is autumn flowering, has softer spines and smaller, deep yellow petals.

**BROOM** *Cytisus scoparius*
North from Hayburn Wyke broom is frequent on heathy cliff tops and beside the disused railway; it can reach 4m high and is usually surrounded by many juvenile plants. Long pliable stems are spineless, evergreen and 5-angled; 1-3 leaflets; flowers followed by flat black pods. Jun-Jul.

**MELILOT** *Melilotus spp.*
**Tall melilot** *M. altissimus* is plentiful on re-graded cliffs as at Scalby and Robin Hood's Bay; branched stems over 1m tall have spikes of deep yellow small flowers, followed by black hairy pods; oval toothed leaflets in threes on short stalks.
**White melilot** *M.albus* often grows alongside; its white flowers produce brown hairless pods. Jun-Aug.

**KIDNEY VETCH** *Anthyllis vulneraria*
Although locally scarce inland it is one of the commonest plants on cliff slopes; bunches of deep yellow flowers each with a white woolly calyx are spread amongst pinnate leaves and stems clad with silky hairs; up to 30 cm tall. Jun-Sept.

**DYERS GREENWEED** *Genista tinctoria*
A rare plant throughout Yorkshire, it has a limited presence on these cliffs northwards from Saltwick. An evergreen shrub, rarely exceeding 60cm, its ridged stems carry short oval leaves, pointed with clear central vein; small pea type flowers. Jun-Oct.

**MEADOW VETCHLING** *Lathyrus pratensis*
Plentiful in grassy ground all along the cliffs; tendrils enable the plant to clamber over other vegetation; large flowers grouped on stalks numerous among grass-like leaves in pairs. May-Aug.

**BIRDSFOOT TREFOIL** *Lotus corniculatus*
Widespread in meadows and on grassy cliffs; yellow flowers with red buds in clusters; <u>solid</u> branched stems spread to 40cm. In damp ground **greater birdsfoot trefoil** is a more upright hairy plant with <u>hollow</u> stems.

**BLACK MEDICK** *Medicago lupulina*
Named from its black coiled fruits; common low spreading plant on turf and rock ledges; small flowers in round heads; leaflets each with tiny end point. Apr-Aug.

**SPOTTED MEDICK** *Medicago arabica*
Locally rare; grows on rough ground beneath Scarborough Castle ramparts and on Ruswarp Batts; flowers small. single and sparse; leaflets with distinctive black spot; dark wheel-shaped spiny fruits. Apr-Sept.

**LESSER TREFOIL** *Trifolium dubium*
Common throughout in short grassland on pathsides and cliffs; low creeping plant with flowerheads only 5-7mm across; leaflets in 3's each with straight or slightly notched end. May-Sep.

**HOP TREFOIL** *Trifolium campestre*
Uncommon winter germinating annual on sandy and waste ground, eg old railtrack; flowers are larger and paler than lesser trefoil; drooping standard petal makes flowerheads resemble small hop cones. Jun-Sep.

**CLIMBING CORYDALIS**
*Ceratocapnos claviculata*
Delicate low scrambler occasional in open woods eg Sycarham near Cloughton and on acid quarry waste; pale lemon/cream cigar-shaped flowers c.6mm long are scattered in a tangle of thin stems, tendrils and small oval leaflets. May-Sept.

**YELLOW CORYDALIS**
*Pseudofumaria lutea*
Similar to the native climbing corydalis, but with larger deep yellow flowers, this Alpine plant escapes to the wild from nearby gardens; not common along the coast; once established it persists on old walls.

## flowers on short spikes

# plantains
*Plantago spp.* have leafy ground rosettes – leaf shape indicates species; unbranched erect pliant stems 10-40cm tall, often called 'rattails', have single spikes of tiny flowers each with 4 long conspicuous stamens, usually yellow or buff; of five local plantains, buckshorn and sea are almost confined to the coast where they are abundant on shore edge, cliffs, pathways; hoary prefers calcareous ground; ribwort and greater are widespread on grass or wasteland.

**GREATER PLANTAIN**
*P. major*
Has large oval deep-veined hairless leaves; greenish stamens on long tough erect spikes. Jun-Oct.

**RIBWORT PLANTAIN** *P. lanceolata*
Has upright leaves, long oval with deep veins; cream stamens and tough flexible stems; very common on cliffs. Apr-Oct.

**HOARY PLANTAIN**
*P. media*
Is unusual in having pink stamens; leaves are broad oval, deep-veined and covered with pale hairs. May-Aug.

**BUCKS-HORN PLANTAIN** *P. coronopus*
Has leaves divided like antlers usually flattened to the ground; bright yellow stamens; common on coast paths. May-Jul.

**SEA PLANTAIN**
*P. maritima*
Has long narrow leaves rather fleshy and upright; stamens pale yellow; common on cliff slopes down to strandline. Jun-Aug.

# flowers on medium to tall spikes

*See also agrimony and mullein, page 56*

**MUGWORT**
*Artemisia vulgaris*
Common on waste ground eg around Whitby harbour; reddish grooved stems over 1m tall carry many deeply lobed leaves dull green above, felted beneath, aromatic; sprigs of tiny yellow/brown flowerheads. Jul-Sept.

**SEA BEET**
*Beta vulgaris*
Frequent on open ground surrounding Scarborough Castle ramparts; scarce elsewhere; large glossy green leaves grow from the base and from reddish ridged stems, often over 2m tall; clusters of greenish/yellow flowers. Jul-Sep.

**MIGNONETTE**
*Reseda lutea*
Occasional on rough ground; branched grooved stems 30-60cm with bushy spikes of small lemon flowers each with 6 petals; leaves deeply divided. Jun-Aug.

*(weld, a similar plant has 4 petalled flowers, simple leaves and is taller).*

**WELD**
*Reseda luteola*
Frequent early coloniser on most cliff slopes; robust plant has grooved stem up to 150cm; upper stems closely packed with tiny yellow/green 4 petalled flowers; leaves narrow, strap-like with wavy edges. Jun-Sept.

**WOOD SAGE**
*Teucrium scorodonia*
Abundant in dry light shade on gravel and shale heaps, especially at Ravenscar; hairy square stems to 30cm; pairs of wrinkled leaves and spikes of small yellowish flowers with prominent brown stamens. Jul-Sept.

**TOADFLAX** *Linaria vulgaris*
Thrives on free draining old rail ballast, especially between Ruswarp and Whitby; flowers with long pointed spur are light yellow with 2 orange swellings on lower petal; short strap-shaped leaves dense on upright stems 30-80cm. Jul-Oct.

### HAZEL
*Corylus avellana*

Only in sheltered woodland does hazel approach tree-size on this windswept coast; as a small shrub it often grows with rose and bramble in scrub or hedge. In early spring, dangling catkins spray yellow pollen onto tiny red brush-like female flowers, later to form hazelnuts; roundish crinkled leaves with wavy edges appear later.

### IVY *Hedera helix*

Widespread on walls and woodsides; evergreen glossy leaves 5 lobed on tough climbing stems – oval on flowering shoots; globes of tiny 5 petalled flowers appear Sept-Nov followed by berry-like green/ black fruits.

### MOSCHATEL *Adoxa moschatellina*
Called townhall clock from the square head which has a flower on each face – and a fifth on the top; a carpeting plant barely 10cm tall; green/yellow flowers appear Mar-Apr through a mat of thin trifoliate leaves in old woodland away from the chalk headland.

### MARSH CUDWEED *Gnaphalium uliginosum*
Small bushy annual with tiny yellow/brown flowers quite frequent in muddy more acidic pathsides, gateways and short grassland; narrow greyish leaves covered in dense woolly hairs; under 20cm tall. Jul-Sep.

---

## spurges *Euphorbia spp.* yellow/green short annuals of dry disturbed ground, frequent on sunny cliffs. Broken stems exude a caustic milky juice; leaves thin, oval almost stalkless; tiny flowers with single stalked ovary lack petals or sepals; may appear any time throughout the year.

### PETTY SPURGE *E.peplus*
Has yellow 'horned' glands; stems reddish, side branches in 2's or 3's.

### SUN SPURGE *E. helioscopa*
Is green/ yellow with tiny bean shaped glands and side branches in 5's; tooth-edged leaves.

**WILD DAFFODIL**
*Narcissus pseudonarcissus*
Grows in deciduous woods around Robin Hood's Bay and at Sycarham wood, Cloughton; shorter and more delicate than the various garden varieties which have been  planted up and down the coast; its narrow yellow trumpet is framed by 6 much paler outer petals. Feb-Apr.

**YELLOW FLAG IRIS**
*Iris pseudacorus*
Occasional in pools and standing water on vegetated undercliffs such as at Blea Wyke, Ravenscar and south of Filey, also in pools at  Cayton and by Sandsend old railtrack; up to 150cm tall stout flower stems; stiff wide leaves with raised midrib. Jun-Jul.

**HAYRATTLE**
*Rhinanthus minor*
Also known as yellow rattle. Rattling of ripe seeds in a dry calyx accounts for the name of this semi-parasitic plant; common on cliff tops and slopes; hairless dark spotted stems 50cm; paired leaves  evenly saw- edged; flowers with violet-tipped top hooded petal and 3- lobed lower petals; flat oval calyx inflates when ripening. Jun-Sept.

**YELLOW ARCHANGEL**
*Lamiastrum galeobdolon*
Rare in old woodland ground flora; from creeping runners erect flower stems to 60cm have whorls of hooded yellow/orange flowers; short  stalked nettle type leaves, often blotched silver, in pairs on square stems. May-June.

**HONEYSUCKLE** *Lonicera periclymenum*
In scrub and hedgerows woody stems with paired oval leaves climb to 6m; at branch ends are several yellow/red trumpet flowers, very fragrant. Jun-Sep; followed by luscious looking but highly poisonous red berries.

**LADY'S MANTLE** *Alchemilla xanthochlora*
This low-growing plant of northern pastures appears infrequently in grassy locations north of Filey where it reaches its south-eastern limit in UK. Named from its cape-like leaf shape, it has bunches of yellow/green small 4-petalled flowers amidst thick foliage. Jun-Sep.

**SEA BUCKTHORN** *Hippophae rhamnoides*
Occasional on undercliffs and often planted eg Cornelian Bay; tiny pale flowers early spring followed by bright conspicuous orange autumn berries; spiny shrub to 3m tall and wide; narrow greyish leaves.

**POPPY** *Papaver rhoeas*
Associated with light calcareous disturbed ground, uncommon along the coast but occasionally spreads from adjacent farmed land; medium hairy stems have single large flowers with 4 papery petals which soon fall.
Jun-Aug.

**MONTBRETIA** *Crocosmia sp.*
A showy popular garden hybrid of South African origin frequent on cliffs even far from dwellings; flower plumes and sword shaped leaves up to 40cm often in large swathes.
Jun-Sep.

**SCARLET PIMPERNEL** *Anagallis arvensis*
Occasional on bare cliff ledges and sandy undercliff; neat oval leaves in pairs along stems; starry flowers close up mid afternoon and in dull weather and have given rise to the name of 'poor man's weatherglass'.
Jun-Aug.

**LORDS AND LADIES** *Arum maculatum*
Fresh green arrow-shaped leaves appear in rich grassy ground from Feb to Apr soon followed by a large papery pointed bract (spathe); this forms a cowl around a green/purple smelly prong (spadix) which attracts pollinating flies; true flowers are concealed in the base; after fertilisation the spadix withers and is replaced from Jul-Aug by bright scarlet poisonous berries clustered on a short upright spike. Occasional on woodside or hedgebank. Also known as cuckoo pint or wake robin.

**RED VALERIAN** *Centranthus ruber*
Often plentiful in retaining walls eg at the foot of Lythe bank near Sandsend and on Scalby promenade; white and pinkish red forms may grow together; small flowers with 5 tiny petals above a long thin tube are massed in bunches; stems and foliage fleshy greyish green.
Jun-Aug.

# clovers

**RED CLOVER** *Trifolium pratense* abundant in grassland; greenish bracts sit <u>close beneath</u> pinkish red globular heads composed of

numerous small pea-typle flowers; pointed oval lealets in 3's usually have pale central mark. May-Sep.

**ZIG-ZAG CLOVER** *Trifolium medium* is similar to red clover but has all green more pointed leaflets and brighter coloured flowers with short bare stem (<u>no close bracts</u>) beneath. May-Sept.

# figworts

*Scrophularia spp.* are large- leaved plants up to 1m tall; small brownish red flowers have one upstanding notched petal and a tiny lower petal. Jun-Sep.

**WATER FIGWORT**
*S.auriculata*
Is quite common amongst rank vegetation on damp cliff ledges; it has square <u>winged</u> stems and toothed leaves with ± <u>rounded</u> tips.

**COMMON FIGWORT**
*S. nodosa*
Grows in shady locations; it has square stems <u>without wings</u> and leaves <u>pointed</u> at the tip.

# burnets

**SALAD BURNET**
*Sanguisorba minor*
Is frequent on drier cliff grassland; small dark red flowers with protruding stamens form a tight <u>globe</u> at the ends of branched stems up to 40cm; pairs of evenly serrated <u>roundish</u> leaflets. May-Aug.

**GREAT BURNET**
*S. officinalis*
Grows sparsely in old pasture on rough grassy cliffs north of Scalby; a large colonial plant with stems to 90cm; <u>oblong</u> flowerheads and <u>oval</u> leaflets. Jun-Sep.

# docks and sorrels

*Rumex spp.* are wayside plants tall with undivided leaves; no petals; green sepals form a triangular base for reddish swellings or 'warts'; leaf shape and number of ripe warts important for identification. Docks and common sorrel have tough ridged stems often over 1m tall; sheep's sorrel is a small plant to 30cm.

### CURLED DOCK
*R.crispus*

Has coarse strap shaped leaves with crinkled edges; stems red tinted; fruits have 3 light red warts on ± smooth-edged roundish sepals when ripe. Jun-Oct.

### CLUSTERED DOCK
*R.conglomeratus*

Grows in rank grassland; zig-zag stem; three oval warts on long sepals. May-Jun.

**WOOD DOCK** *R sanguineus*
Similar to above but has straight stem, prefers damp shade and fruits have only one round wart. Jun-Aug.

### BROAD-LEAVED DOCK
*R.obtusifolius*

Has wide blunt pointed leaves, edges uneven but not crinkled; ripe fruits have 1 large deep red wart with two undeveloped warts between fringed sepals. Jun-Oct.

### SHEEP'S SORREL
*R. acetosella*

Grows on impoverished ground eg shale heaps, rail ballast; shorter than other rumex species, it has small oval leaves each with 2 projecting 'tailfins'; fruits without warts; leaves turn scarlet in late summer. 10-30cm.

### COMMON SORREL
*R. acetosa*

Is plentiful on cliff tops; leaves long thin arrow-shaped, once gathered as a flavouring herb; reddish sepals have no warts. 30-80cm.

### REDSHANK
*Persicaria maculosa*

Common annual weed of arable and damp ground; narrow hairless leaves have dark centre blotch; reddish stems swollen with fringed stipule at leafstalk joint; 70cm. Jun-Oct.

### PALE PERSICARIA
*Persicaria lapathifolia*

Similar to redshank and often growing alongside but not as numerous; flowers greenish white; lower stipules not fringed. Jun-Oct.

# willowherbs
*Epilobium spp.* – a large family with many species and hybrids; all have pointed oval leaves and long stem-like fruits which split to release ripe 'parachute' type seeds; each flower has a central stigma either club or cross shaped; this is a useful identification guide along with petal size and colour also habitat and size of plant. Only the locally most frequent species are shown.

## cross stigma

**ROSEBAY WILLOWHERB**
*Chamerion angustifolium*
Common, forming large colonies on old quarries, rail tracks and rough grassland; large flowers have uneven sized petals, <u>cross</u> stigma; this hairless tall plant, now country wide was a British rarity 2 centuries ago. Jul-Sep.

**GREAT WILLOWHERB**
*E. hirsutum*
Colonising plant covers large areas on seeping cliffs; hairy leaves and stems to 150cm tall; flowers with 4 notched matching bright pink petals, <u>cross</u> stigma with recurved lobes. Jul-Aug.

**BROAD-LEAVED WILLOWHERB**
*E. montanum*
Frequent in light shade on disturbed ground; leaves almost hairless but flower capsule softly downy; pale notched petals, <u>cross</u> stigma; 20-60cm tall. Jun-Aug.

**HOARY WILLOWHERB**
*E. parviflorum*
Is similar to great willowherb with a <u>cross</u> stigma but is shorter and has smaller paler flowers; hairy foliage gives greyish look; scattered in damp places; 30-60cm. Jul-Sep.

## club stigma

**AMERICAN WILLOWHERB**
*E. ciliatum*
Was introduced in 1890 and is still spreading; has small deeply cleft pale mauve petals; <u>club</u> stigma; glandular hairs on reddish stems to1m tall. Jun-Aug.

**MARSH WILLOWHERB**
*E. palustre*
Is a slender 15-60cm plant of acid wetland; <u>club</u> stigma in small flowers; strap-shaped smooth edged leaves. Jul-Aug.

**SEA ROCKET** *Cakile maritima*
Sandy shores at Sandsend and Cayton have fluctuating populations of this driftline annual; seeds dispersed by tides; fleshy stems and lobed leaves on sprawling plants; lilac flowers. Jun-Aug.

**CUCKOO FLOWER** *Cardamine pratensis*
Limited by scarcity of wet meadows; fringes slow moving streams; on 25-60cm stems open sprays of pale mauve flowers appear at the same time as cuckoos are calling; also called milkmaids. Apr-Jun.

**DAMES VIOLET** *Hesperis matronalis*
Large mauve or white flowers with delicate evening fragrance, garden plant naturalised on waste ground and cliffs near habitation; large oval toothed leaves on tall stems; fruits long, narrow tubular; grows in clumps. May-Jul.

**HONESTY** *Lunaria annua*
Infrequent garden escape differs from dames violet by large flat ± circular silvery fruits and triangular leaves curved around the stem; faintly fragrant. Apr-Jun.

**FIELD MADDER** *Sherardia arvensis*
On short non-acid turf and disturbed soil this spreading prostrate plant flowers all summer from May; small tubular pale lilac flowers in groups amongst long green bracts; square trailing stems and leaves in whorls of 4-6 have short end points.

**AUTUMN GENTIAN** *Gentianella amarella*
Also known as felwort, a frequent annual of grazed lime-rich turf and dunes but scarce on this coast; occasional on cliffs between Runswick and Hayburn Wyke; stems to 30cm with pairs of dull green pointed leaves have purple/pink flowers; 4 or 5 pointed petals open wide above long narrow calyx tube. Aug-Sept.

### CENTAURY
*Centaurium erythraea*
Widespread in small scattered groups on cliff slopes; a neat plant with starry shell-pink flowers on stems 10-30cm; hairless oval leaves with parallel veins clasp the stem in pairs; often grows with yellowwort (p58) – both are members of the gentian family. Jun-Oct.

### SEA MILKWORT *Glaux maritima*
Mat-forming prostrate plant of upper sandy shores at Cayton and Sandsend, marsh at Ruswarp Batts and on rocks at Filey Brigg; short erect stems are packed with pairs of fleshy leaves which partly hide tiny pink flowers. Jun-Aug.

## cranesbills
*Geranium spp.* Plants with open flowers usually on short paired stems; tapered fruit resembles bird's beak; when ripe it splits into 4 sections which coil backwards to disperse myriads of seeds.

### DOVESFOOT CRANESBILL *G. molle*
A carpeting plant with soft hairy leaves and stems; numerous small pinkish-mauve flowers Apr-Sep; common in dry short grassy places.

### BLOODY CRANESBILL  *G. sanguineum*
Mainly a plant of well-drained lime- rich soils; on this coast known only on lower cliffs at Primrose Valley where it grows with sawwort (p79) also locally rare; large crimson-mauve flowers single on long stems; bushy plant up to 60cm. Jul-Aug.

### CUT-LEAVED CRANESBILL
*G.dissectum*
A well-named species with leaves cut into short linear segments; hairy low-growing plant frequent on grassy or bare ground; small deep pink flowers. May-Aug.

### HERB ROBERT
*G. robertianum*
Familiar strong-smelling plant frequent on disturbed or rocky ground from cliff top to shore and in gardens; flowers all summer; stems and deeply cut ferny leaves often reddish; petals not notched; 10-40cm high.

### STORKSBILL
*Erodium cicutarium*
Frequent on sandy turf at Flamborough; spreads close to the ground; leaves sticky .hairy; flowers have unequal petals with upper 2 often black spotted at base; beaked fruit twists open to expel seeds. Jun-Sep.

# roses are a complex group of plants with numerous hybrids showing a range of species characteristics.The two main local groups are described. Garden cultivars are quite frequent. (*See also white-flowered burnet rose page 36.*)

### DOG ROSE *Rosa canina*
Is plentiful in cliff top scrub and undercliff thickets; long tough stems, large hooked prickles, <u>shiny green</u> serrated leaflets in pairs; pink/white flowers to 5cm across Jun-Jul.

### DOWNY ROSE
*Rosa mollis*
Has bright pink petals, <u>greyish downy</u> leaves and mostly straight prickles; not as widespread as dog rose but single bushes occasional in hedgerows. Jun-Aug.

### JAPANESE ROSE
*Rosa rugosa*
Is an ornamental garden shrub quite common on cliffs near caravan sites; arching spiny stems have <u>shiny wrinkled</u> leaves, dark pink flowers, large hips. Jun-Jul.

### RAGGED ROBIN
*Lychnis flos-cuculi*
Each of 5 petals deeply notched into 4 uneven segments giving flowers a ragged appearance; med-tall plant occasional in wet grassland and undercliff marshes. May-Jun.

### MALLOW *Malva sylvestris*
Widespread large bushy plant frequent in arid habitats eg around Sandsend car park and exposed cliffs; 5cm flowers produce tyre-shaped fruits; leaves said to soothe a wasp sting. Jun-Sep.

### RED CAMPION *Silene dioica*
Tall hairy colonial plant usually on humus-rich wood edge or bank; abundant on sea-bird cliffs at Bempton; 5 petals deeply notched may appear as 10. Mar-Oct.

# spurreys *Spergularia spp.* are low spreading plants with linear often fleshy leaves and flexible growth form which assists survival in salty habitats and under frequent sea inundation. On tidal mudbanks of R.Esk between Whitby and Ruswarp, often growing together, are two sea spurreys. Both have also been found in the splash zone of heavily salted roads.

### GREATER SEA SPURREY
*S.media*
Pale pink flowers c.10mm across.
Jun-Aug

### LESSER SEA SPURREY
*S.marina*
Deep pink flowers 6-7mm across.
Jun-Aug

*see p36 for white-flowered corn spurrey*

**orchids** are widespread and numerous on grassy cliffs and conservation meadows; shape of flowerhead and lower lip of single flower help to identify species; leaf-spotting and colour are variable. (*See also frog orchid and twayblade in green section page 47.*)

### COMMON SPOTTED ORCHID
*Dactylorhiza fuchsii*
Has ± cylindrical head; flowers blush white to deep pink, lower lip with darker dots and loops has projecting centre lobe. Jun-Aug.

### HEATH SPOTTED ORCHID
*Dactylorhiza maculata*
Is usually pale pink; lower petal marked with dots and streaks; small centre lobe equal to or shorter than side lobes; prefers acid heathland; infrequent on moorland edge.

### FRAGRANT ORCHID
*Gymnadenia conopsea*
Slightly triangular slender spike; fragrant soft pink unspotted flowers have long thin spurs hanging down; leaves narrow, keeled with few markings; Jun-Jul; favours dry lime-rich soils.

### PYRAMIDAL ORCHID
*Anacamptis pyramidalis*
Has short pyramid-shaped head; lower petal edge has 3 similar rounded lobes; rose to dark pink petals with white centre. Jun-Aug.

### BEE ORCHID *Ophrys apifera*
Appears erratically on cliffs from Sandsend to Flamborough in both old rank grassland and on re-aligned cliff slopes; fleshy stems 15-50cm tall have up to 6 multicoloured flowers; a brownish 'furry' lower lip resembling a female bumble bee attracts pollen-laden male bees as pollinators. Jun-Jul.

### BROAD-LEAVED HELLEBORINE
*Epipactis helleborine*
Occurs infrequently amongst leaf litter in shady old woodland around Fylingthorpe, Staintondale and Hayburn Wyke; muted pink/bronze/greenish flowers; stout stems clasped by broad oval pointed leaves. Jul-Oct.

77

# orchids (cont)

### EARLY PURPLE ORCHID *Orchis mascula*

Can be numerous in wooded gullies and on moist undercliffs; stout spikes 15-50cm tall; spur on deep purple flowers points upwards; upper petals form a hood and 2 erect wings; leaves have elongated dark blotches. Apr-Jun.

### NORTHERN MARSH ORCHID *Dactylorhiza purpurella*

Despite its name this quite short stocky orchid thrives in grassy areas as well as in moist ground; nearing its south-eastern limit in Britain at Flamborough; leaves spotted near tip; flowers wine-purple with diamond-shaped, dark- streaked lower lip. Jun-Jul.

# valerians

*Valeriana spp.* have small tubular 5-lobed flowers held in dense sprays on erect med-tall plants. (*See also red valerian page 70.*)

### MARSH VALERIAN *Valeriana dioica*

Occasional in damp ground; runners create clumps of up to 60cm tall stems topped by dense sprays of small pale pink flowers, male and female on separate plants; lower leaves long-stalked and spoon-shaped. May-Jun.

### COMMON VALERIAN *Valeriana officinalis*

Infrequent in rough grassy areas; stems reach 120 cm; sprays of small pinkish flowers, male and female on same plant; all leaves lobed or divided into toothed leaflets. Jun-Aug.

# fumitories

*Fumaria spp.* are spreading plants with hairless waxy foliage and slender stems; tubular flowers have 2 outer petals with tiny spur near the stalk and dark tips; small round fruits.

### COMMON FUMITORY *F. officinalis*

Grows on arable fields along cliff edges, occasional on drier cliff slopes; low tangled clumps of weak hairless stems; greyish finely dissected leaves; spikes of pink cigar-shaped flowers 6-8mm long. May-Oct.

### RAMPING FUMITORY *F. capreolata*

Has flowers c.10-12mm long, cream with dark mauve tips; broad leaf segments; a vigorous scrambler over ground and high up hedges; common around Lythe and northwards. May-Sep.

### SMALL SCABIOUS
*Scabiosa columbaria*

Frequent on cliffs from Cayton to Flamborough; heads 2-3cm wide have larger florets round the edge; black bristles in calyx beneath; hairy stems to 70cm; leaves finely divided. Jul-Sep.

### FIELD SCABIOUS
*Knautia arvensis*

Needing well-drained calcareous ground, not common north of Flamborough; robust hairy plant to 1m tall; flowerheads 3-4cm across; 2-rowed calyx; coarse divided leaves. Jul-Sep.

### DEVILS-BIT SCABIOUS
*Succisa pratensis*

Scattered on grassy cliffs; the curious name arises from roots which appear 'chopped off'; globular flowerhead 2-3cm across; pointed oval leaves not divided; 10-40cm pliant stems. Jul-Oct.

### COMMON KNAPWEED
*Centaurea nigra*

Very common on cliff grass-land; tough grooved stems to 60cm are branched with a single flowerhead; hard blackish calyx . Also called hardheads or black knapweed, not to be confused with brown knapweed which is confined to southern UK. Jul-Sep.

### GREATER KNAPWEED
*Centaurea scabiosa*

A lime-lover frequent on Flamborough cliffs, occasional elsewhere; a handsome plant up to 1m tall has large showy flowerheads; deeply notched long outer florets give an open 'raggy' appearance. Jun-Aug.

### SAWWORT
*Serratula tinctoria*

Infrequent in small groups on a few vege-tated under-cliffs eg Hunmanby and Upgang ravine; differs from knapweed by its saw-edged linear leaflets and narrow elongated flowerheads; smooth striated calyx. Jul-Sep.

# thistles
Robust prickly plants 50-100cm tall, in flower between Jul-Oct. *(See also carline thistle page 60.)*

### CREEPING THISTLE *Cirsium arvense*
Widespread in rough grassland; stems furrowed, ± spineless towards the top; flower-heads held in close groups; florets pale mauve; grows 30-90cm tall, often in large stands. Jul-Sep.

### MARSH THISTLE *Cirsium palustre*
Stem and leaves short spined, flushed red; much branched stem to 2m tall; a spindly plant with clustered flowerheads; common on damp cliff slumps. Jul-Sep.

### SPEAR THISTLE *Cirsium vulgare*
Spiny woolly stem to 150cm; leaves large with long yellow-tipped sharp spines; forms robust branched bush; common in rough ground. Jul-Oct.

### WOOLLY THISTLE *Cirsium eriophorum*
Grows on Knipe Point, Osgodby, rare elsewhere; large round woolly single flowerhead on strong spiny stem to 150cm; leaves felted beneath. Jul-Sep.

### WELTED THISTLE
*Carduus crispus*
Widely branched uncommon plant with dark flowers and foliage; leaves pale felty beneath. Jun-Aug.

### SLENDER THISTLE
*Carduus tenuiflorus*
Frequent around Staithes; spindly, greyish plant; stem has <u>wavy spine-edged wings</u>. Jun-Aug.

### MUSK THISTLE
*Carduus nutans*
Grows sparsely at Ravenscar and Flamborough; large nodding heads very fragrant. May-Aug.

## HEMP AGRIMONY
*Eupatorium cannabinum*
Frequent large colonies on undercliff seepages often with fleabane and common reed; tiny florets dense on tall stout stems; large toothed leaflets have 3 or 5 lobes. Jul-Sept.

## TEASEL *Dipsacus fullonum*
Occasional on cliffs; ridged spiny stems up to 2m; large prickly flowerheads with long spiny bracts. Jul-Aug. Formerly cultivated for carding in woollen cloth manufacture.

## BURDOCK *Arctium minus*
Common on tracksides or in scrub; sturdy bushy plant to 130cm with rhubarb-shaped coarse leaves; heads of dull mauve florets with hooked bracts which assist seed dispersal. Jul-Sep.

## UPRIGHT HEDGE PARSLEY
*Torilis japonica*
Common roadside plant occasional on cliff tops; flowers Jul-Aug after cow parsley; tiny notched white or pink petals; rough solid dark stems to 1m high, widely branched; ferny dull foliage.

## THRIFT
*Armeria maritima*
Tiny 5 petalled flowers in 'posy' bunches on 15cm stems; short grass-like greyish leaves; abundant on Flamborough cliffs, scarce elsewhere. Apr-Aug.

## MARJORAM
*Origanum vulgare*
Fragrant bushy plant of dry calcareous soils eg re-aligned cliffs and Flamborough headland; many paired sprays of tiny flowers. Cultivated as a culinary herb for its aromatic leaves. Jul-Sep.

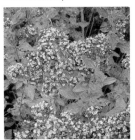

## BUTTERBUR *Petasites hybridus*
Extensive on shallow stream banks; short buff stems appear in March, produce sprigs of packed dusky pink flowers to be followed by foliage; leaves mature to nearly

1m broad and last all summer. Formerly used as cool wrappers for butter.

## FRAGRANT BUTTERBUR *Petasites fragrans*
Known as winter heliotrope in gardens, this short leafy plant continues to colonise road verges eg Burniston, Sandsend and cliffs at Holbeck; vanilla scented

flowers in Jan soon hidden by carpet of roundish leaves; 10-25cm tall.

### HOARY PLANTAIN *Plantago media*

Long pink stamens separate this species from other coastal plantains (*see page 66*); small groups on cliff tops and slopes away from rank vegetation, usually on lime-rich soil; whitish hairs on stem and leaf give this plant its hoary look. 4 -10cm. May-Aug.

### WATER MINT *Mentha aquatica*

Strongly aromatic colonies spread around cliff pools and rivulets, often with meadowsweet and fleabane; small 4-petalled mauve flowers with projecting stamens form <u>oval</u> clusters at stem tops. Jul-Oct. (garden mint or spearmint flowers in <u>spikes</u>).

### BISTORT *Persicaria bistorta*

Occasional in damp ground; projecting stamens on tiny flowers Jun-Aug; stems to 1m; hairless leaves tapering into long stalks. **Amphibious bistort** has narrow leaves like those of redshank (*see page 72*); uncommon.

### BRIDEWORT *Spiraea salicifolia*

A garden shrub naturalised at Reighton and Staintondale; large bushes of willowy stems up to 2m long; small bright pink 5-petalled flowers on tapering leafy spikes. Jun-Jul.

### PURPLE TOADFLAX *Linaria purpurea*

Originally a garden plant, now established in sheltered locations near habitation; attractive spurred purple flowers on tall stems with numerous short grass-shaped leaves; pink-flowered forms may grow alongside. Jun-Aug.

### PURPLE LOOSESTRIFE *Lythrum salicaria*

This lowland pond and canal plant has established by a small pool on Cayton shore; square stems up to 1m tall carry loose whorls of 6-petalled reddish-purple flowers; lower stems have whorls of 2 or 3 large pointed leaves. Jun-Aug.

*Have 5 petals comprising an upright 'standard' at the top, 2 'wings' at the sides; 2 lower petals making a 'keel'; vetches and vetchlings have leaves divided into 2-12 pairs of narrow pointed leaflets.*

**EVERLASTING PEA**
*Lathyrus latifolius*
Brightly coloured garden plant naturalised north of Sandsend where it clambers extensively near the sealed tunnel on the old railtrack. Jun-Aug.

**BUSH VETCH**
*Vicia sepium*
Up to 6 dusky mauve flowers and 3-9 pairs of blunt leaflets which diminish in size towards the tendrils; frequent in grassy scrub; up to c.50cm. Jun-Aug.

**BITHYNIAN VETCH**
*Vicia bithynica*
Upgang ravine is its only confirmed site in north east UK; trailing winged stems; fringed stipules; 2-3 pairs of pointed leaflets; few flowers. May-Oct.

**WOOD VETCH** *Vicia sylvatica*
More frequent on the coast than inland; climbs high in trees and scrub; delicate mauve striated flowers; up to 10 pairs of even sized leaflets. Jul-Aug.

**TUFTED VETCH** *Vicia cracca*
Commonest coastal vetch; scrambles 2m high; up to 40 small deep blue/mauve flowers and 8-12 pairs of narrow leaflets. Jun-Aug.

**BITTER VETCH** *Lathyrus linifolius* Infrequent on acidic grassland; upright plant to 40cm; 2-4 pairs of long narrow leaflets, no tendrils; flowers age through pink/cream/blue. Apr-Jul.

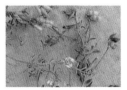

**TARE** *Vicia spp.*
Unobtrusive low scrambling plants with tiny drab bluish mauve flowers; **Hairy tare** *V.hirsuta* has small hairy 2-seeded pods; scattered on old railtrack and bare ground, frequent alongside Whitby's 199 steps to the Abbey; **Smooth tare** *V.tetrasperma* has hairless 4-seeded pods; rare in the north, grows near Ruswarp.

**COMMON VETCH**
*Vicia sativa*
Scattered but nowhere abundant despite the name; 4-8 pairs of narrow pointed leaflets; 1 or 2 deep mauve flowers in leaf axils above fringed green stipule which has a <u>dark centre spot</u>; low-med plant. Apr-Sep.

**RESTHARROW**
*Ononis repens*
Common low spreading shrublet may have spines; white and pink forms often together; toothed oval leaves sticky-hairy; stems to 60cm <u>hairy all round</u>. Jun-Sep; (**spiny restharrow** (O.spinosa), an upright long-spined plant with <u>2 rows of stem hairs,</u> has not been been confirmed on this coast).

# moorland shrublets

### HEATHER
*Calluna vulgaris*
Moorland tough shrublet common between Ravenscar and Stoupe Beck, small patches on acid soils elsewhere; flowers mauve, narrow bells on short twiggy spikes; leaves densely overlapping in short flat rows. Aug-Sep.

### BELL HEATHER
*Erica cinerea*
Small shrubs create large colonies on dry shale in old alum quarries eg Deepgrove; flower bells pear-shaped, deep purple/ mauve; leaves dark green with edges rolled under, in small whorls spaced on flowering stems, clustered on others. Jun-Sep.

### CROSS-LEAVED HEATH
*Erica tetralix*
Prefers damp acid peat which is sparse on the coast; flowers light mauve bunched at stem tops; leaves hairy, in 4's up stems, have pale underside almost concealed by rolled-under edges; fruits downy. Jun-Sep.

### BILBERRY
*Vaccinium myrtillus*
An open small shrub of acid heath, scarce on the coast; green twiggy angular stems to 60cm have deciduous oval toothed leaves and small rounded bell flowers Apr-Jun; tasty deep blue berries ripen Jul-Aug, often gathered for pie or jam making.

### CROWBERRY
*Empetrum nigrum*
Infrequent spreading low plant of drier moorland; wiry stems with  needle leaves tightly rolled back to expose only a whitish streak of underside; miniscule petalless flowers in leaf axils May-Jun are followed by more visible bitter black berries.

### FIELD BINDWEED
*Convolvulus arvensis*
Persistent and widespread scrambler on rough ground and scrub; long twisting stems have ± triangular leaves and stalked large trumpet-shaped flowers, pink streaked white. Jun-Sep.

**FOXGLOVE** *Digitalis purpurea*
Handsome biennial plant of acid soils; occasional on wood edge or scrub; from stout stems over 1m tall hang up to 80 bell flowers, mauve with spotted interior; large soft hairy leaves have winged stalks. Jun-Aug.

**COMFREY** *Symphytum spp.*
Tall robust plants in large clumps on verges and rough grassland; flower colour varies according to species; coarse leaves once used to poultice broken bones; now valued for making a rich, if pungent, liquid fertiliser. Jun-Aug.

**LOUSEWORT** *Pedicularis sylvatica*
In Scarborough castle grounds and occasional on damp grassy cliffs; short hairless plant with small ferny leaves; flowers with large lip and toothed hood protrude from angular pointed calyx. Apr-Jul.

**RED BARTSIA** *Odontites vernus*
Often overlooked pathside plant; small dull pink flowers spaced up short stems, partly hidden by small hairy pointed leaves. Once used to relieve toothache. Jun-Jul.

**HIMALAYAN BALSAM** *Impatiens glandulifera*
About 160 years ago this was a new garden treasure; its prolific spread in the wild now threatens natural wetland vegetation – eg along the River Esk at Ruswarp; flowers up to 4cm have 2 large lips and small spur; seed far flung by noisy exploding capsules; large pointed leaves on 2m tall branched stems cast dense shade. Jul-Oct.

**DEADNETTLES** *Lamium spp.*
**Red deadnettle** is common on most short grassy or bare ground; pinkish mauve flowers in whorls near tops of square hairy stems up to 40cm; dull green wrinkled leaves often reddish; flowers most of the year; **cutleaved dead-nettle** has more deeply toothed leaves; a less frequent plant of arable land.

**BLACK HOREHOUND**
*Ballota nigra*
Occasional in rough ground; loose stands of hairy leafy stems; drab mauve flowers white- streaked; coarse acrid smelling plants up to 1m tall. Jun-Oct.

**WILD BASIL**
*Clinopodium vulgare*
Faintly aromatic plant of dry calcareous scrub, locally rare; hairy paired leaves; pink flowers in sparse whorls; branched erect plant to 80cm. Jul-Sept.

**CALAMINT**
*Clinopodium ascendens*
A lowland hairy plant of base-rich scrub, rare in the north, survives on Scarborough castle ramparts; square stems to 30cm; mint scented. Jul-Sep.

**BUGLE** *Ajuga reptans*
A colonial plant of damp ground occasional on wood edge and cliff seepage; deep bluish/purple flowers on bronze stems; lower lip white streaked; differs from selfheal by its glossy leaves and lack of upper hooded petal. Apr-Jun

**SELFHEAL** *Prunella vulgaris*
Common short plant covers patches of grassland and wayside; squarish packed flowerheads of purple hooded flowers top erect stems throughout summer; dull hairy leaves contrast with shiny smooth leaves of bugle; May-Oct.

**BETONY** *Stachys officinalis*
Widespread on cliff top grassland especially in conservation meadows eg Hunmanby. Differs from other mauve/pink lipped flowers by its compact flowerhead and neatly serrated blunt-tipped leaves. Jun-Oct.

**GROUND IVY** *Glechoma hederacea*
Low spreading plant frequent on well-drained ground; winter-green roundish leaves softly downy, crenate-edged; also known as 'alehoof' – formerly a beer brewing ingredient. Flowers Mar-May.

**HEDGE WOUNDWORT** *Stachys sylvatica*
Occasional in less shaded parts of wooded gulleys and moist hedgebanks; bristly 1m tall stems with loose whorls of dull reddish mauve flowers; despite a pungent smell, the leaves have antiseptic qualities valued by ancient Greeks through to the present day. Jun-Oct.

**WILD CLARY** *Salvia verbenaca*
A few of this aromatic sage-type plant linger precariously on ramparts of Scarborough castle; a rare species north of East Anglia. Flowers drab purple on spikes above rough branched stems 30-80cm tall; coarse crinkled leaves. May-Aug.

**TOOTHWORT** *Lathraea squamaria*
Parasitic short plant feeding mainly on roots of hazel or elm; infrequent in old woodland eg Hayburn Wyke; flesh-coloured stubby spikes have given rise to the name of 'dead man's fingers'. Apr-May.

**PELLITORY OF THE WALL** *Parietaria judaica*
Widespread around Whitby where it may have been used medicinally by Abbey monks; it thrives in wall mortar; reddish stems to 70cm have small clusters of tiny drab flowers; oval leaves softly hairy. Jun-Oct

**BUTTERWORT** *Pinguicula vulgaris*
Distinctive upland plant of bogs and wet rock ledges occurs infrequently in undercliff flushes, eg Blea Wyke and Flamborough; nutrients are absorbed from insects trapped by sticky glands on yellowish ground rosette leaves; erect stems to 10cm have spurred flowers. May-Jul.

**WILD THYME** *Thymus polytrichus*
Mat-forming aromatic plant of dry heathland infrequent on rocky outcrops on coastal cliffs; tough creeping square stems hairy on 2 sides only; tiny mauve flowers amidst pairs of small hairy oval leaves; cultivated forms used as culinary herb. May-Aug.

**SMALL TOADFLAX** *Chaenorhinum minus*
A small annual once common in cornfields, appears erratically on old railtrack and quarry waste; stem and short leaves hairy; tiny dull mauve flowers have short spur. May-Oct.

**IVY-LEAVED TOADFLAX** *Cymbalaria muralis*
A rock garden plant now frequent around villages in wall mortar and in gravel eg Filey promenade in front of cabins; small spurred lilac flowers have a yellow spot to attract bee pollinators. May-Sep.

**BITTERSWEET OR WOODY NIGHTSHADE**
*Solanum dulcamara*
Appears erratically on lower cliffs sometimes at shore level; sprawling plant; distinctive bright flowers produce red oval berries which taste bitter at first then sweet but can cause sickness if eaten.

**DUKE OF ARGYLL'S TEAPLANT**
*Lycium barbarum*
A greyish shrub with long spiny branches and suckers which penetrate hedgerows and walls in a few places eg Staithes, Hawsker, Whitby; bright purple starry 5-petalled flowers Jun-Sep mature into long oval red berries.

**violets** flowers with 2 upper and 3 smaller lower petals. Sepal and leaf shape help identification. (*See also pansies on page 56.*)

**DOG VIOLET** *Viola riviniana* Common in light shady woodland and open pasture; heart-shaped long-stalked leaves; flowers have squarish outline (unlike early wood violet); deep violet petals contrast with <u>pale cream stout spur notched</u> at the end; sepals <u>pointed</u>. Mar-May.

**EARLY WOOD VIOLET** *Viola reichenbachiana* Occasional in deciduous woodland; differs from dog violet by its narrow elongated flower face and <u>dark violet slender spur not notched</u>; sepals <u>pointed</u>; flowers from early March usually a week or two before dog violet.

Both wood and dog violets have pointed sepals

**SWEET VIOLET** *Viola odorata*
Occasional in light shade near paths; flowers white or deep purple and fragrant; slightly hairy heart-shaped leaves; rooting runners cause flowers to appear scattered over large patches. Mar-May.

**HAIRY VIOLET** *Viola hirta*
Similar to sweet violet but less common; flowers are scentless and bluish purple. As the plant lacks runners its flowers grow in dense clumps, not scattered.

**MARSH VIOLET** *Viola palustris*
Uncommon creeping plant of acidic wetland grows on cliffs at Ravenscar and Robin Hood's Bay; pale lilac striated flowers often hidden by vegetation; cordate leaves resemble ice cream cones when young. Apr-Jul.

Both sweet and hairy violets have <u>blunt sepals</u> and prefer lime-rich ground. Mar-May.

# speedwells

Veronica spp. are low-med plants with opposite leaves, 4 unequal blue petals, the lowest often paler; 2 prominent stamens and a heart-shaped rather flattened fruit; species are adapted for various wet and dry habitats; some flower throughout the year. Location, leaf shape and colour are helpful for identification.

### FIELD SPEEDWELL
*V. persica*
Common on field edges and bare ground; flowers long stalked; leaves in pairs, yellowish green, toothed, almost round.

### GERMANDER SPEEDWELL
*V. chamaedrys*
Creeping hairy plant widespread on grassy banks, tracksides; short upright reddish stems have 2 distinct lines of pale hairs; flowers strong blue with white centre.

### BROOKLIME
*V. beccabunga*
Common in shallow freshwater and on damp tracks where it can form extensive mats of succulent hairless foliage; flowers bright blue.

### THYME-LEAVED SPEEDWELL
*V. serpyllifolia*
Widespread in bare or short grassy ground; flowers pale blue with dark lines; hairless oval leaves with strong centre vein and almost stalkless.

### WALL SPEEDWELL
*V. arvensis*
Widespread on walls and dry ground; erect or prostrate stems with tiny deep blue flowers; dark green paired leaves coarsely toothed.

### SLENDER SPEEDWELL
*V .filiformis*
It is less than 100 years since this garden plant spread to the wild; now frequent in mown grassland; small rounded leaves, faintly toothed.

### IVY-LEAVED SPEEDWELL
*V. hederifolia*
A low spreading plant of rather dry ground, woodside or waste; pale mauve/blue flowers; small hairy leaves ivy-shaped.

### WOOD SPEEDWELL
*V. montana*
Infrequent on woodland edge; creeping plant with yellowish/green leaves; stems hairy all round; flowers pale lilac.

### HEATH SPEEDWELL
*V. officinalis*
A hairy widespread often patch-forming perennial on dry heath and wood edge; short spikes of small pale flowers have lilac striated petals.

# forgetmenots

*Myosotis spp.* have small open powder blue flowers with 5 equal roundish petals, yellow centres; oval leaves usually softly downy; coiled flower spike unfurls as buds open.

*in dry ground:*

### FIELD FORGETMENOT

*M. arvensis*
Is the most frequent species, plentiful on dry disturbed ground; <u>flowers saucer-shaped 5mm</u> across; forms extensive loose clumps. Apr-Oct.

### CHANGING FORGETMENOT

*Myosotis discolor*
Has tiny flowers which change from yellow to blue as they mature; occasional on bare light soils. May-Jun.

### WOOD FORGETMENOT

*M. sylvatica*
Is a plant of woodland shade; like field forgetmenot but with <u>flatter flowers up to 10mm</u> across; brighter blue. Apr-Jul.

*in marshy ground:*

### WATER FORGETMENOT

*M. scorpioides*
Spreads in freshwater margins; it has bright blue flowers up to 10mm across; petals notched; calyx teeth broad and shallow. May-Sep.

**TUFTED FORGETMENOT** *M. laxa*
Is scattered in marshy places; soft blue flowers only 4mm across, May-Aug; long narrow calyx teeth; hairs <u>pressed close</u> to the stem.

**CREEPING FORGETMENOT** *M. secunda*
Creeps in shallow acid water; short hairs at <u>right angles</u> to stems; flowers 6-8mm on long stalks which bend over as fruit matures; long narrow calyx teeth. May-Aug.

## *composite flowers*

### SEA ASTER

*Aster tripolium*
Saltmarsh plant occurs sparsely on tidal shores of R.Esk Whitby to Ruswarp; dusky blue/mauve flowers; erect branched stems c. 40cm; fleshy hairless narrow leaves. Jul-Sept.

### CHICORY

*Cichorium intybus*
Appeared recently on re-structured cliffs at Robin Hood's Bay. Showy plant to 1m tall; groups of large blue/mauve flowers on tough hairy stems which are clasped by pointed lobed leaves. Jun-Oct.

**GIANT BELLFLOWER**
*Campanula latifolia*
Infrequent handsome plant of woodland edge or hedge-bank; groups of tall erect stems carry large open bell flowers, bluish mauve; large spear-shaped serrated leaves. Jul-Aug

**BLUEBELL**
*Hyacinthoides non-scripta*
Plentiful in wooded valleys and cliff scrub; several long bell-shaped fragrant flowers hang on one side of fleshy stalk (garden variety has upright bells facing all ways). 20-40cm. Apr-Jun.

**HAREBELL**
*Campanula rotundifolia*
Delicate plant frequent in short grassland on cliffs and waysides; slender blue bell flowers hang on thin waving stems; roundish lower leaves soon wither; later linear stem leaves persist; up to 40cm. July-Sept.

 # milkworts *Polygala spp.* Quite frequent on short grassland, especially between Speeton and Flamborough; prostrate stems trail amongst other vegetation; flowers c.5mm long, tube-shaped, can be blue, pink or white; small oval leaves with deep central vein are alternate along the stem of **common milkwort** *P. vulgaris*; they are in opposite pairs on lower stems of **heath milkwort** *P. serpyllifolia*. May-Sept.

**GREEN ALKANET** *Pentaglottis sempervirens*
A robust garden plant occasional in clumps on cliffs near villages; its small 5-petalled deep blue flowers give no hint of the red dye obtained from its roots; coarse deep-veined hairy leaves on bristly tall stems. May-Nov.

**MEADOW CRANESBILL** *Geranium pratense*
A blue-flowered lime-loving geranium infrequent in rough grassy areas on the coast; prominent bushy plant to 80cm tall has pairs of saucer-shaped flowers up to 4cm across; sticky hairy stem and large toothed leaves. Jun-Sep.

## INDEX of scientific names

## FURTHER READING

New Atlas of the British Flora initiated by the Botanical Society of the British Isles and published by Oxford University Press in 2002 *(a comprehensive survey of all British plant species with maps showing their current and historical distribution; includes CD ROM)*

Wild Plants and their Habitats in the North York Moors by Nan Sykes; published by the North York Moors National Park in 1993 *(a local survey of vascular plants with maps showing the distribution of most species)*

New British Flora of the British Isles by Clive Stace; published by Cambridge University Press in 1991 *(a complete classification and botanical description of all British plant species)*

Wild Flowers of Britain and Ireland by Marjorie Blamey, Richard Fitter and Alistair Fitter published by A & C Black Publishers Ltd in 2003 *(a detailed, fully illustrated, identification and distribution guide to British and Irish wild plants)*

Field Guide to the Wild Flowers of Britain published by the Readers Digest Association Ltd in 2001 *(a well illustrated identification guide to most British wildflowers)*